THE WIL

THE AUTOBIOGRAPHY

THE WILD ROVER
THE AUTOBIOGRAPHY
OF
TOMÁS Ó CINNÉIDE

Translated into English
by
PÁDRAIG TYERS

MERCIER PRESS

MERCIER PRESS
PO Box 5, 5 French Church Street, Cork
and
16 Hume Street, Dublin

Trade enquiries to CMD DISTRIBUTION,
55a Spruce Avenue, Stillorgan Industrial Park, Blackrock, Dublin

First published in Irish, *Ar Seachrán*, in 1982.
ISBN 1 85635 182 3

10 9 8 7 6 5 4 3 2 1

A CIP record for this book is available from the British Library.

A NOTE FROM THE TRANSLATOR
Because the original Irish language version of this book was spoken unrehearsed on tape by Tomás Ó Cinnéide I have attempted to translate it into the kind of English which I feel a man like Tomás would have used had he been telling his story in that language.

I am deeply indepted to An Canónach Dónall Ó Ceallacháin for his extremely valuable advice and suggestions all through the time I was engaged in the translation.

Printed in Ireland by Colour Books Ltd.

CONTENTS

1
A Child is Born

My Ó Cinnéide ancestors came from Ballinahow, a sheltered place to the north in the Parish O' Moore in West Kerry. They went from there to Ballynabuck in the same parish and that is the townland where my father was born. He had three or four brothers and five sisters, if I am not mistaken.

When my father was growing up to be a fine strong young man he and his brother Micheál, known as An Cúl, left home just like the young chick departs the nest when the feathers and wings come. They hoisted their sails but didn't go very far. They took the road east for a half-mile or so and settled in Cuas which was a fishing harbour at that time. It is still a fishing harbour, but I'm afraid there is no fish being caught there now. My father built a grand cosy little house there, and they lived and fished together as happy as could be. An Cúl had paid a flying visit to America and came home with the same boots he was wearing when going there. That shows that he didn't stay long there because he wasn't at all inclined to work.

After a while my father got an idea. It was a natural one too, to get married. Not surprisingly he didn't wish to have the brother in the house with him after marrying. Of course it wasn't that he had any dislike or hatred for him. Not at all. Indeed the very opposite was the case, so he said to himself that he would set the brother up first.

He had heard that a girl of the O'Connors had come home from America to Graigue, about twelve miles away to the western side of the parish of Ballyferriter, as indeed she had. It was decided that my father would go to Graigue to make a match between her and An Cúl. Soon afterwards he set off west on foot. He paid a visit to a couple of 'watering places' on the way because he believed that a few drinks would be a great help in giving him courage. He called into Feohanagh, I am told, and after Feohanagh he called into Ballyferriter. I suppose he knew the publicans there but whether he did or not he was welcome if he had a shilling, and a shilling was worth a shilling in those days.

It was well into the evening when he reached Graigue. O'Connors' house had a thatched roof. The door was wide open. He went in. There were two women inside, one of them an old lady sitting in the corner writing her name in the ashes with her stick, if what they say is true, and the other a good-looking girl with hair halfway down her back, busily doing her work around the house.

Before either of the two women had time to say 'Lord save us!' my father had spoken. 'Is it here the man is needed?'

The old woman looked at him. 'It is indeed,' she said with a touch of sarcasm. 'It is a man we want and not an idler, whoever you are.'

My father introduced himself. The old woman's words didn't deter him.

'It is like this,' he said. 'I have a brother at home who is anxious to marry and I hear that ye are looking for a son-in-law to come into the house.'

They listened to what he had to say and the beginning and end of it was that they decided to go to Dingle on a particular day to make the match. That was how it was done in those days. Matches were made in Dingle so that the neighbours would not know anything until the matter was settled. My father left and headed home for Cuas very pleased with himself, but he had not gone far when another thought struck him. Quite possibly he stopped in the middle of the road because that thought was a very serious one. He said to himself, and maybe he said it out loud: 'She is too fine a girl, and I'm damned if I'll ever give her to the brother. I'll marry her myself.'

That is what happened. The brother stayed in the house in Cuas, the match was made for my father and he married Máiréad Ní Chonchúir in Ballyferriter on Shrove Tuesday 1905. I am told that there was a number of weddings there the same day. That is not surprising because in those days nobody married during the rest of the year. The world and his mother were in the village. You could hardly get into a public house because after a wedding all you did was to make for the nearest one. The people were very loyal, and so if there was a pub with which you had any connection that is where you went. I am not saying that you wouldn't call into the others, if you felt that way inclined. Then having finished with Ballyferriter you would bring home a barrel or two or three, or maybe four, if you could afford them.

There were great celebrations in Graigue when my father and mother came home after their wedding. It was a night until morning. The following day my father got the notion to go into the Western Island on their honeymoon, whatever affinity or tie he had with the people there. They weren't thinking of the Hillgrove or of Benner's Hotel, if such places existed at all then.

I am told that they spent the best part of a week on the Island. What a grand place it was then, full of people and fine people at that.

After their stay in the Island they had to return home and look after the big old cow they had. I suppose my father thought that he had come in for the big farm in Kilnagleragh. Maybe he was losing the run of himself when he bought two more cows, which he shouldn't have done because I think myself that the holding was too small and too barren. The only fertiliser available in those days was the one from the strand, the seaweed, and that is what killed the land in Graigue and in other places as well.

Anyhow my father's marriage was the start of the Ó Cinnéide clan in Graigue, and it was as a result of it that myself, my five brothers and three sisters were born. They all lived until they were grown-up except one, Breandán, who died when he was only a child, and I have a feeling that he was far better off dying than living the sort of life I have lived.

Three great events took place in the year 1914 and that is a long time ago now. In the first week of the month of August, I am told, the First Great War broke out, the war that was supposed to end all wars. On the twentieth day of the same month St Pius X, Pope of Rome, died, and in between on the fourteenth I was born.

There was nothing unusual about my coming into the

world, because many a person had come before me and will come after me too, except for one thing – there was a great night's fun in Graigue that night.

There were two women taking care of my mother. They were from Clogher, aunts of my father. They came up on to the main road on their way to Graigue. One of them had a rope under her arm. A neighbouring man met them. They saluted one another. 'Where are ye going with the rope?' the man asked.

One of the women answered sarcastically: 'We are going to Graigue to pull a calf.'

That was all there was to it. The man wasn't left any the wiser, and he had no earthly idea until the following day what sort of calf had been born. Anyway it is said that just as I was coming into this sinful world my nose was squashed. Signs on, it is as it is, and I don't know how to describe it. But that is how it happened. I didn't get it from fist-fighting.

My father was out fishing. That was his livelihood because it would have been useless for him to be depending on whatever bit of money he might make out of the land. When he came home he was told that a young son, a fine lump of a fellow, had been born to him. As you might expect he was proud as punch just as any father would, and he wanted right go wrong to see him. But the old women from Clogher were well able for him. They told him that he would have to have patience and wait until the following day to see him. He insisted that he would have to see him straightaway and told them why. 'About a fortnight or three weeks ago,' he said, 'I dreamt that I would have a young son and that I would call him after myself,' which he did. 'And as well as that I dreamt that he would have a cross on his back.'

The women started laughing at . him. They had good reason to do so because it baffled them why in the name of heaven a father would say that his son would be born with a cross on his back, but he told them that this particular son would be a bishop. Years later when I was grown up I was telling some people the story and one of them said to me: 'Your father was right in a way. The cross was on you, sure enough, but it wasn't a bishop's cross but the cross of an ass!'

There's sarcasm for you!

A couple of days after I was born my father put the horse under the cart and sat in. My godmother Máire de Londra from Ballincolla sat in too, with me in her arms to bring me east to Ballyferriter to be christened. We weren't long reaching our destination. The horse was untackled. My father and god-mother went into the chapel, and of course so did I.

The priest knew we were coming. He was An tAthair Mac Seoin, or Fr Jones as everyone called him. He was very famous as he had been a great handballer and musician and athlete. After a little while he came out to us. He looked around. Then he spoke. 'Where is the godfather?' he said.

'I haven't one, Father,' said my father innocently.

'Well if you haven't,' he said, 'get someone. Go out and get a man to stand for the child or if you don't the child will go home again just as he came, a pagan.'

My father went out. At that very moment it just so hap-pened that Tomás Mac Gearailt from Gortmore, a short dis-tance west of Ballyferriter, was passing the chapel gate with a load of sand from the strand. My father went over to him. 'For God's sake, Tomás,' he said, 'tie the animal and come in with me fast because I have no godfather to stand for the child that is to be christened.'

They went in. The job was done. I was baptised and came out a Christian. We went home but if we did it wasn't without a drink or two, because on the day of a wedding or christening people would have to have a drop wherever they would come by a pound.

2
CORK BOOTS

According as I was growing up and getting bigger I used to watch my older brothers and sisters slipping out the door every morning on their way to school in Ballyferriter. I used to cry as I watched them going off while I had to stay at home full of cheek and impudence, with no company except for the youngest lad Séamas who was just a year old and still crawling around the floor. As well as that it was a real scald for my father and mother to have the likes of me under their feet because I know I was troublesome from childhood. In the latter end they had to let me off with the others and so I headed east with them. That was the year 1920. I wasn't much more than six years old.

But, alas, mad and all as I was for the road I regretted it afterwards. In the first place the journey was very long for a child like me, three miles exactly from the house to the school, and another thing, because I was in the infants' class I used to be let out at half-past two whereas my brothers weren't allowed out until half-past three. So there was an hour between us and because I didn't know the road home I had to wait until they came out. But help came my way because there was a boy across the road from us, Tomás Ó Conchúir – he was the same age as myself except that I was a few months older – who started going to school soon after me and was in the same class as I was. We were companions from that day until death took him when he was only eighteen years, may God have mercy on his soul.

High spirits made me want to go to school at first but I soon found out that it entailed a lot of hardship, especially because of our diet and the way we were dressed. All we had to eat in the morning was bread and a drop of tea. Most people in those days were dependent on the sea, their two oars and their two hands, but the sea is like a cow that produces only when she feels like it, and the poor people here were often hungry when the fish, not to mind the money, ran out. If you had a shedful of potatoes and two barrels of salted fish you wouldn't be afraid of any winter be it hard or mild. But, alas, many is the time we had no fish and then the only tasty thing we had was the pickle, or 'dip' as English speakers called it. If you had milk with a grain of salt in it you dipped your potato into it – it really was tasty – you filled your stomach, and out you went.

We had no such thing as boots, not like today when a child has boots on him coming into the world almost. We went to school barefoot, some of us anyhow, in the very heart of the winter. I remember how, when there was ice on the ground, we used to put stones under our backsides and race one another as we slid down from the little fields above the house. Our legs were full of sores from the frost, but like every other change that has come over the world in the last fifty years there is never any frost here nowadays like we used to have long ago. Or maybe there is and it is melted before I leave the blankets, because I don't feel a bit like getting up during the cold. I have seen my best days and have neither calf nor cow to drive out to graze, so I am free to stay in bed until late into the day.

My brother Micheál thought of a plan and said that we would make our own boots. Corks were very plentiful in every fisherman's house because the mackerel nets were full of them. We got two corks each and used to put them under the soles of our feet with a twine around them. Then we would tie them on the backs of our legs without any stockings and hit the road to school. We used to take the shortcut east along the top of the fields, and on coming out on the road again at Seán Teaimí's gap in Teeravane we would take off the corks, put them into the schoolbag and walk barefoot east through the middle of the village and past it. Then we would put them on again until we got as far as Ballyferriter West. There a feeling of shame would come over us again for fear people might see the children from Graigue going to Ballyferriter School wearing cork shoes and so we would take them off again.

We were carrying on from day to day and year to year, growing up and advancing from class to class. The first teacher we had was Liam Ó Lúing, or Willie Larry Long as we usually called him. Willie had his own way of teaching and was very nice to young children. But his class was anything but a kindergarten because Willie, and many others besides, didn't know the meaning of the word. Then we went to Pádraig Ó Briain's class and finally I had Micheál Ó Conchúir, who was the principal since the first day I went there. By the way his son Doncha, who was a classmate of mine during part of my time at school, is now the principal.

Our family stayed together the same as any other family until misfortune struck and the scattering began. One by one we left home to face the great world outside.

My eldest brother Pats was the first to leave and went off to San Francisco six thousand miles away. He was about eighteen or nineteen years of age then. He had spent a couple of seasons fishing, but he left the fishing behind him and with good reason, because after the lucky escape he and an old man from Clogher had in Coosnanay once when their little canoe was broken in two halves he knew he was in danger of being drowned any day he went out fishing.

I'll never forget my mother's crying and wailing when Pats was leaving, just as if he was being waked. She was all the time saying that she would never again see him even though he was only a young man. Other people, especially a first cousin of hers who had come to the house on the previous night, tried to get her to stop crying and said that he would soon come home again to see her. However my mother's prophecy that she would never see him again turned out to be correct.

The horse was tackled – we had a black horse at the time – and whatever luggage Pats was taking with him was put into the cart. He sat on the left-hand side, my father sat on the right, and of all the children in the family who were going to school that day I was the one who sat in with them. They were going to Dingle to catch the train, and before they dropped me at the school gate Pats promised to send me the price of a bicycle from America if I stayed on at school and gained whatever benefit I could from it. I jumped out of the cart, shook hands with him and went into school.

After Pats went west to San Francisco we used to write to

each other. I always wrote to him in Irish, although I wasn't too good at writing letters at that time, but like all the other native speakers of Irish who went to America he always wrote in English to myself and my mother, though to my mind he had no English because when we were growing up there wasn't a word of English to be heard west of Ballyferriter except that English was taught in school for a half-hour each day.

At home we were so short of everything including money that we had no notepaper, but I wasn't short of a plan. When the pupils were let out of school in the middle of the day our own teacher would go home for something to eat because his house was very near the school. If I was thinking of writing a letter to America after going home that evening I would slip into the teacher's room while he was out. I knew where the box was in which he kept his notepaper because he used to write a lot of letters. I would take a page or two, put them into my pockets, bring them home and write to my brother.

Pats never sent me the price of the bicycle, I'm afraid, nor the price of anything else either, because he had gone away that time to a country that was torn asunder by poverty and as badly off for money and work as the country he had left behind. When I shook hands with him that day outside Ballyferriter School little did I think that I would never again see him, because he died over in San Francisco when he was only thirty-five years old.

In my time there was a battalion of children going to Ballyferriter School from this townland and from Clogher. We were in time hardly any morning because instead of hurrying to school we were always up to some devilment, and in those days if you were five minutes late, no matter what excuse you had, you weren't listened to. You got the stick, and we certainly did. There was always one day, though, when we had a very good excuse. That was the day of the Stations. We still have the Stations and I hope they will never be allowed die.

The curate, An tAthair Ó Loingsigh, used to come into the school from time to time. Whatever he knew about music he would comment on our singing. He told the master one day – I heard the words myself – that I would make a great singer yet, I above all the boys and not a note in my head!

I well remember the kind of pastime we had nearly every afternoon coming home from school. We, the boys from Clogher, and those from Teeravane maybe, if they had courage enough to stay with us, would wage a war of stones on the lads from the other side of the parish, from the slopes of Bally-oughteragh and Gortadoo and Ballincolla. It was a very dangerous pastime and I realise it more now than I did then. If we had any sense we would hit the road home instead of playing with deadly weapons, because if you got a rock in the forehead or in the eye you would have reason to cry. Youth is like that. The stones on the road were not sharp. They were large, and plentiful too. Of course there was no tar on the roads then. It wasn't even thought of. If the likes of us were there today they couldn't go throwing stones because there are no longer any loose stones on the road.

There isn't a child that doesn't like sweet things and it was the same with us. We would go under the wheel of a cart to get sweets, but there was no way of getting the money except by stealing the odd few eggs. We were a holy terror. We hardly left our mothers any eggs. We would steal them, hide them in a hole in the fence, bring them to Ballyferriter the next morning, sell them for a penny each, and buy sweets with the money. A penny was a lot of money in those days.

Another thing that I myself longed for ever since I was ten or twelve years old was a bicycle, but there wasn't a hope of getting it for except for the postman nobody in the parish had one. He always believed in taking the world fine and easy and I don't blame him. It was his custom to go into a certain house in the neighbourhood nearly every day and have a smoke at his ease. While he was inside I would come along unknown to him and take the bicycle until he had finished his smoke. When he came out I would jump down off the bicycle and throw it aside. He would rush after me but the poor fellow was never cross. He only let on to be because he was a likeable easy-going man. That is how I came to have such a longing for a bicycle.

One day when I was about thirteen or fourteen years old I went off walking across Murreagh Strand to Kilcooly in the parish of Keel to visit my aunt, a sister of my father's. She was married there to an O'Dowd man. A son of hers was studying for the priesthood in Louvain in Belgium at that time. I stayed with her for a couple of days, and this particular day when I was getting ready to come home she called me aside and said to me : 'Tomás, there is an old bicycle belonging to Pádraig inside here and I don't think anyone will ever make any use of it. If you think you can repair it take it away home with you.'

My heart jumped with joy. I threw the bicycle up on my shoulder because it had only one wheel. I was indeed a funny sight walking home barefoot across the strand. Before I reached Ballinrannig on this side of the strand I heard a noise to my right and I looked out towards the mouth of the harbour. Above the Black Rock I saw the bird, as I thought, coming in towards me and heard a queer sound up in the sky that I had never before heard from anything. I stopped and gazed in wonder and amazement. What was it only an aeroplane, and who was in it only Lindbergh himself coming all on his own from America, the first man ever to do so from New York to Paris in France! He was directly over my head. I was so delighted that I raised my hand by the way to salute him and I imagine that he saluted me too! But of course he wasn't walking and he hadn't his bicycle on his shoulder either. That is how it was. I was going west and Lindbergh was going east and each one of us was just as happy as the other. That was the 21 May 1927.

When I reached home I got down eagerly to repairing the bicycle, but I'm afraid I never rode it because I didn't have the parts to put it in working order.

It so happened that there was a girl from Cork named Máire Ní Luasa on holidays in MacSwineys' house in Graigue around the same time, and she knew the longing I had for some sort of an old bicycle of my own. She promised to send me one on the Dingle train when she got back to Cork. A week or fortnight later a postcard arrived telling me that the bicycle would be in Dingle station this particular day, and I'll never forget the words on the card: 'I have put new brakes on it,' she said, 'for fear you might kill yourself.'

The bicycle arrived. I walked to Dingle for it and got it in the station. I was all excitement when I saw it. There was never anyone in the world as happy as I was that day. And talk about the jealousy and envy it caused later on when I used to bring it with me to Ballyferriter School! The first bicycle ever that any boy or girl had going there came from Graigue, but if so it wasn't Graigue money that bought it.

Myself and other lads like me were mad on football too. We would give our right hand from the shoulder down to have a football, but like that and the story we were often without one, eager and all as we were for it. In those days we used to get a football when the potatoes were being dug at the end of the year, and were still on the ground or maybe in bags in the field. A gang of us would go out at night-time with three or four empty bags and before the end of the night those bags would be filled, tied with twine and hidden away, ready to be brought to Dingle and sold on the side of the street. Whenever we heard of any of the neighbours going to Dingle with a cart we would throw in a bag or two and sit in with him. With that money we would send for a football over to Birmingham in England of all places. Three shillings and sixpence it used to cost. It always arrived pumped up and, oh God of Graces, wasn't youth wonderful? How delighted we always were to see the postman coming with the ball on the front of his bicycle. It was easy to see it because it was always white in colour. We would run half a mile to meet him, and before we got a chance to lay our hands on the ball he would get off his bicycle and give it a lash in over the fence so that he could boast that he was the first to get a kick at it. We would jump in after it without any permission whatsoever and play away until the owner of the field came along in a temper. Then we would have to run off somewhere else.

We grew up going to school and back again and progressing from class to class. With the coming of summer every year the biggest boys and girls would have to stay at home. They had no business at school because there was nothing to be gained from being there even if they stayed two years in eighth class. The girls used to go into service. That is the term we used when a girl left home to work as a domestic while still only twelve or thirteen years old. The boys would go fishing for a year or two maybe. Then they would get tired of it and head off across the sea.

In those days boys and girls from the Gaeltacht, or Irish-speaking area, could do an examination before the age of fourteen, and if you were successful you got a scholarship and could go to a Preparatory College and continue on until you became a schoolmaster or schoolmistress. I was well capable of doing so myself. An Máistir Ó Conchúir knew I was intelligent enough to win a scholarship, and he called me aside this particular day to tell me that he would like to see me get on. While we were talking – maybe he had paper and a pen in his hand ready for action – he asked me what age I was. I told him.

'Oh my,' he said, 'what a pity! You're two years too old.'

I was trapped. I had no choice but to stay where I was for a while longer.

After another few years there was hardly anyone else from Graigue or Clogher left at school except myself, and I spent two years in eighth class simply because there was nothing for me to do at home. I was very fond of school and the books were no great problem to me. I understood what was going on. I know very well that I had a smattering of English leaving school because I still have words and sentences in my head that I got in the books which we had. There was one very nice book which I have never come across since, *A Swordsman of the Brigade*. There were many words in it that we didn't understand but the teacher was always at his level best trying to teach us and we managed. In my second year in eighth class there was nothing on the school programme that I hadn't done and so the teacher gave me a job as monitor teaching the young pupils. Every afternoon after school I used to drop into the village post office and do odd jobs for the woman of the house, the best woman who ever broke bread. I might bring her a bucket of water from St Brendan's Well just west of the village, say, and so on and so forth. I used to get a drop of tea and a slice of bread from her and going home I felt as if there wasn't a poor person among my relations.

I stayed at home from school for five or six months until I got the idea of going and talking to the Christian Brothers in Dingle. I was accepted by them and told to come to school whatever day I liked. I had the bicycle at the time but unfortunately Dingle was twelve miles away and so the bad weather often kept me at home because I had no overcoat. However there was a guard in Ballyferriter who had a sister-in-law. Whatever way she became aware of my problem didn't she give me two coats of her own! When going to Dingle on bad mornings, as was often the case, I would wear the two coats with a twine around me to tie them. Only for that I could never have completed the year's course which I did there.

I never came home at all on bad evenings because it was the will of God, and I am thankful to him for it, that I got to know a grand man who was living alone in a small house in the Colony back near the Pier End. His name was Lar Kaye, a very holy man, and it was because of his holiness and charity that he took me in. He never ate a bit of meat, whether he had the price of it or not, nothing but fish which he used to get for nothing from the boatmen. He had only one bed in the house and the two of us slept together in it. Lar never wore a stitch of clothes in bed. That was a common habit amongst the old people in those days because they loved it like that. They used to say, not just to themselves but to the whole wide world, that sleeping without any clothes was a sign of cleanliness.

That is how I spent the last couple of years of my life in school until I stayed at home for good, and you can take it from me that I was almost a man at that time. I was seventeen or eighteen years old if I am not greatly mistaken.

3
YELLOW-ASH TURF

Some people would say that I never did a day's work, wherever they got that idea, and I may as well leave it at that now because they will have peace of mind if I say that they are right. I wasn't altogether as bad as that, however, and signs on I am living on my money now. Only for the small amount of work which I did I would not have any income or means today. Neither would I be in Graigue but in the poorhouse, and there is such a house in Killarney that would gladly take me in.

I admit that I didn't do much work when I was in Graigue but then I didn't have to. I had a brother Seán – the Lord have mercy on him, he is dead and buried – and anybody who is still alive and remembers him knows that he was the most hard-working man that ever took a spade in his hand. My father was just as hard-working.

Once in a while I would go out to them while they were working. Usually we had only three cows and a couple of big stubborn calves, and that meant that we didn't do much tillage. One day my father was ploughing furrows down by the sea within a field of the Old Ground. He told me to guide the horse for him. I was always full of devilment and so, instead of staying in the furrow and taking the horse by the head, what did I do but jump up on his back! My father was bare-footed guiding the plough, and there was I, the little ruffian, with my two pockets full of pebbles trying to hit him on the toes. In his innocence the poor man didn't know where the shots were coming from and he kept asking me, 'What's hitting my feet?'

It was nothing new for my father to be barefoot, because in those days when the summer heat and sun came the old people loved to throw off their old boots, not because they were poor but because that was what they were used to since their childhood. That was how they preferred to be, especially when working in the fields because the boots were very heavy. I remember one man from Ballinrannig – he is with the God of

Glory this long time – a very religious and very charitable and very good man, who used to come to Ballyferriter without boots even when he was an old man. The women too went barefoot most of their lives.

I used to cut a bit of turf sometimes but when the turf was being saved I was usually given the task of footing it and then gathering it for my father while he made the rick. There was never any real turf in Graigue, only top-sod, of which there was plenty on Minnaunmore and Clogherhead. However, before we began to cut turf on Minnaunmore or Clogherhead we used to go to Farran where there were two kinds of bog. There was turf there called yellow-ash turf, or *drom bán* in Irish. We used to get that for nothing because we were closely related by blood and marriage to the owner – he was married to my father's sister. We would save that turf and bring it home to Graigue but no one could stand the smell of the ashes. It was unhealthy. There was the second kind of turf too, hard black turf, but you had to pay the owner of the bog if you wanted to take away a load of that or cut a rick there. The turf was always cut by my father and Seán.

This particular morning during the time of the Black and Tans my father went west to Clogherhead to cut top-sod with his spade in the place called the Headland of the Skulls. He had a live sod of turf in an old tin and the purpose of that was to light his pipe because there wasn't a match to be got for love nor money in those days.

He put a couple of sods together with the live ember in the middle and it wasn't long until he had smoke and fire. There was a gale of a wind blowing and you could see the smoke a half-mile away just as two lorry-loads of Black and Tans came eastwards by Toonakilla from Dunquin. When they got as far as the bend of the road at Graigue they had to stop because the IRA had cut the road in two places a short distance from one another. Worse still, as well as the road being cut, huge big rocks had been thrown out on to the middle of it. The Tans got out of the lorries. They looked around and the first thing they saw was the smoke. They started whistling and beckoning to the man with the spade in his hand cutting the top-sod. Of course the poor man was as innocent as St John the Baptist about the whole thing. Still and all he came over to them. He had no choice. They asked him what he was doing with the fire and who cut the road. He said he didn't know. The first thing they did was to make him roll the stones in against the fence. He nearly killed himself doing so. They then accused him saying that he was in fact preparing a meal for the IRA who were hiding among the rocks back at Clogherhead. That certainly was not the case and he told them so. They did nothing but set upon him and proceed to hit and belt him with the guns on the shoulders and on every other part of his body until he fell in a weakness. They left him there, backed their lorries and went their way.

Someone brought word to the house that the poor man was on his last legs back at the Bend of Graigue, as indeed he was. Help was sent for and people came willingly. They brought a door back with them and carried him home on it. He was put into bed and although I don't remember it – I was very young at the time – he spent six months on the flat of his back in bed without earning a pound or even a half-sovereign for his family. It seems that he was injured inside because he was vomiting blood.

I spent most of my time in Graigue knocking around while the others were working. I used to travel from place to place, as far as Smerwick and Kilcooly and Ballynabuck twelve miles away to see my relations, but that was only an excuse to be on the go. I went to a certain house in the Parish O' Moore once. I was closely related to the man of the house. He asked me to stay because they were up to their eyes in work saving the corn. The job I was given to do was to gather the sheaves and face their bottoms into the wind. In those days that was done before making stooks. The bottoms were often green and wet because sometimes there was chicken-weed through the corn. Six sheaves were gathered together and put on top of one another with their lower ends facing into the wind. In the evening they were stooked and tied.

I spent a week working there but then the day of the currach races in Ballydavid came and the sledge-hammer of the foundry wouldn't stop me from going there. For what I thought was a week's hard work what thanks did I get in terms of money? Sixpence! Some fortune! But to be on the safe side I won't say who the man was. 'Let not our enemies hear us', as the man who said it said.

I wasn't at all like my father as far as work was concerned. He was a stocky man. He wasn't tall or bony but, as he himself used to say, he was made of real stuff right back to his tail-end. He worked from dawn until dark but as far as I remember he didn't gain much from his labours. His favourite work was breaking stones. Wherever he found a stone, be it in a field or a garden, he would go around it, dig four feet under it and put gelignite into it to blast it. He had a sledge-hammer – in fact he had two – and because he was so fond of them he was nick-named 'The Little Sledge' and that name stuck to him until the day he died. He was often soaking wet outside in the rain, but that work wasn't of much benefit to him because there was nothing to be got out of breaking stones, but at least he was clearing the land and building fences. As proof of that the fences are still there, some of them twelve feet high.

He and my mother were always sparring. A lot of the work my father did inside and outside failed to earn him any thanks from my mother. Instead she would make game of him and they would often have a go at each other. My father was a very patient man. I suppose you could say he was a saint. He had no ill-will or bad feeling towards any living soul. Any-thing he could do for you he would do it with a heart and a half. He was very religious. He had two prayer-books and I still have one of them, whoever I give it to when I leave this world. I am almost certain that he wasn't able to read much in any language. Still he was able to read the prayer-books.

There was no earthly chance that he would miss Mass, and you would be surprised at how earnest he was in God's House during it. Of course the Mass in those days was very different to the Mass we have today, because no matter how fast you might be you couldn't read the prayers of the Mass long ago in the time that it takes nowadays. My father always went to Ballyferriter Mass when he was young, but then according as he was getting on in years he went to Dunquin because it was nearer. The Mass in Dunquin was at twelve o'clock and that left him with plenty of time to spare in the morning. However he was always fasting from midnight.

Our parish priest, An tAthair Tomás Ó Muircheartaigh, may God increase his glory in heaven, was very slow saying Mass. Not only was he slow with the Mass but the sermon would last over an hour. He wasn't always talking about the Holy Spirit or the God of Glory either, but about this world, and giving the people advice. He used to say that it was far better for a person to drink the drop of milk from his cow than to send it to the creamery because that person was only wronging himself by selling the milk instead of putting it into his stomach. I suppose it was his innocence that caused him to say things like that because he was very old by then.

As for my mother you would swear by the Holy Bible that there was contempt in every word and sentence she spoke but that was not so. There was a touch of the poet in her and she was a wonderful speaker of Irish. She was far more fluent than my father, a gift which she inherited from her mother Cáit Ní Mhainnín from Kildurrihy. Every time I was sent to Kildurrihy on messages forty years ago and more I felt that the most fluent speakers I ever met lived there. Whatever words of Irish I have I think Cáit Ní Mhainnín is the person who should get the credit, as well as my mother of course, because Cáit died when I was still a child in petticoats.

We were poor, very poor, still we survived, thank God. While my father worked outdoors or fished my mother minded the house. If you got up out of bed in the middle of the night for any reason, a cow calving or some such thing, more than likely she would be up at the head of the table with a light beside her, patching or sewing a garment belonging to me or to someone else. She was very elegant and very loving and kind-hearted, as were all the other neighbours around us. She was very patient too, particularly with me after I had grown up.

Most of our clothes came to us from Dingle, but if so they didn't come from the dearest shop in the town. We kept away from such shops because if a poor person went into a shop that had the name of money and grandeur they would nearly tell him to get out. On fair-days every month two or three cars would come from Tralee and halt above at the top of the street. When those dealers held the secondhand clothes up in the air and called out the prices you could hear them shouting east in Annascaul. Then you would hear one voice, two voices, three voices: 'Come down, come down a shilling or two!' and in the latter end the bargain was made.

That is how my mother, and many other mothers besides, bought our clothes and sometimes they would bring home a cart-load depending on the amount of money they had to spend.

Graigue was a wonderful place in those days. There were six houses there. The Ferriters, Seán and Muiris and their mother Máire Thomáis, lived in the next house below us, but not a stone of their house is to be seen today, nor any trace of the site. The two O'Sullivan families were a little to the east of us and then there was the Kevanes' house, the farthest east of all and a short distance up from the road. One of the O'Sullivan families lived above our house at one time and I believe they moved east the year I was born. The O'Connors were near us too until they moved down across the road that same year. I suppose my coming into the world was the reason that they all moved so fast!

I clearly remember the grand people that lived in the townland. Of course when I say that I'm not faulting or running down the people living there now. Many is the night late and early I recall a knock on the door or on the window and one of the neighbours in distress calling on my mother for help, and not only my mother but every other mother and every other housewife as well. People called to them about some urgent problem, the birth of a calf, perhaps, or even a child, because in those days every woman was a midwife. Even though they hadn't much education or read many books they had a knowledge all their own. I remember a couple of houses that had no clock, and it didn't bother them very much either. There is no house without a clock today. The doors were never shut, and even during the night some of them were wide open. There was neither a bolt nor a lock on them inside or outside. That was Graigue in those days. The same was true about Clogher, the townland nearest us. We were very close and very friendly with them, as well as being related to them. But I am afraid that things are no longer so. You wouldn't feel like going to bed nowadays with your door wide open because of the number of people without house or home going the road, particularly in the summertime. The old world has passed and the new one has arrived. When I was a youngster the people of Graigue had their own faith and their own wisdom and they would put you thinking. I asked one of them one day: 'Do you believe in God?'

'Why wouldn't I believe in Him?' he said.

'Why do you believe in him,' I said, 'and why are you so sure that the like of him exists?'

'Listen,' he said, 'who made Clogherhead? Don't you know well that it wasn't some fellow with a shovel or spade that made it? And who laid out the White Strand and put the sand there? Don't you know that no human being did it?'

I don't know if the young people of today think at all of the great miracle around us, to mention only the sight of the Plough and the North Star on a fine moonlight night, or even when there is no moon. The old people were very innocent, so innocent indeed that one of them said that the world wasn't going around at all because if it was the Great Raven Rock would have disappeared long ago, and the Little Raven and the Great Sound and the Little Sound and every other sound as well.

'But,' said he, 'I have been here for the last eighty years and I'm looking out today and I'm seeing now the very same thing that I saw forty years ago. If I were to be alive a thousand years from today I don't think the Raven would have moved, and it never will.'

The old people suffered hardship and trouble and hunger but they gladly accepted it all, the poor creatures. But though I say so maybe I myself and others like me are the ones who are poor, even if we had thousands and thousands of pounds. They are rich because I know they are with God in heaven.

They had to endure hardship every day of their lives ever since the oldest of them was in petticoats, and some of them lived to be ninety. Still they were much happier than the people of the present day who have money to burn. They went into a pub only the odd time. They would have a little drop the day they went to Dingle, especially the day they brought home the Christmas fare, and it is true that very often they brought home very little because they couldn't afford it. If they got a pig's head and pig's feet – things that you wouldn't see at all nowadays because the young people wouldn't consider them fit for eating – they were fully satisfied and thanked God the same as they thanked him for the hardship that came their way. Not a day came that they didn't go down on their two knees that night and say the Rosary.

I am not saying that they didn't become bitter now and again. Some of them did. That was their nature. Some others didn't because it wasn't their nature. They all believed in God and in his Mother and never lost heart no matter what their predicament. Even when death came they accepted it because it was the will of God.

When I was in the army I recall getting word that my brother Pats had died in America. When I got as far as the town of Dingle on my way home my father, brother and sister were there to meet me. As you can understand I began to cry on seeing them but I'll never forget my father's faith when he said: 'It was God who gave him to us and it was God who took him away from us. We are thankful to his will. Let us do his will and we will be all right.'

4
FORTY-ONE

The people in Graigue had their own pastimes. At night during the winter and into the month of April everyone went rambling to some house or other in the townland. It was the same in every townland. There was some house where people always gathered. Many of them used to gather into our house. We children used to be around the floor in the middle of the house playing our own games. The women used to be by the fire, three or four or five of them maybe, chattering and making the devil's own noise. As the old saying goes, 'A flock of geese or a flock of women'.

Live Splinter was the game we usually played. We would shove a splinter into the fire and then pass it on from one to the other while it was alight, and these were the words we said:

Live splinter, dead splinter,
Conked out and fell to ground!

Then everyone jumped down on top of the fellow in whose hands the splinter died as he said the words. It was a strange game, for all the world like the rounders we used to play out in the field. I am told, whether it is true or not, that those same rounders were very similar to baseball, the national game of America that millions of pounds are spent on every year.

Everyone looked forward to the night-time, especially those who were fond of cards. There were great card-players in the parish. They were second to none. As soon as they finished eating the last bite and the night fell they started playing. That was the only pastime the grown-ups had. They had no time at all for us, still they couldn't say a word to us because our mothers were there and we would catch hold of their tails if anyone said anything to us.

In some houses they began playing at six o'clock, in others about seven. There were eight players. Forty-one was the usual game and the stakes weren't very high, I can assure you. Usually they were no more than a penny a game, but a penny was often the cause of a row, especially when they found out that somebody had reneged. That means not playing the card that should have been played. Some of them would have only two pence starting off and hoped to come away with four. Four pence was a lot of money because if you bought, say, a penny-worth of sweets in those days you would get an amount of them, but really what the old people wanted was a plug of tobacco, not sweets, and they could get an ounce of tobacco for four pence.

They didn't always play for money, however. They often played for a sheep, and a sheep was very cheap. She mightn't even cost eight shillings, that is a shilling a man. A pig's head was very often the prize. Sometimes they didn't have the money to play for the second pig's head. The pair who won it would get the sharpest knife in the house and make two even halves of the head, and so each of them would have a half-head going home after the night, delighted with himself, and looking forward to coming the following night and having another half-head going home.

There was nothing the card-players hated more than having somebody standing behind them as they played. These people were known as prompters. You weren't allowed to open your mouth unless you were involved in the game and if you as much as said one word you were told straightaway to move off, because there were only eight players and it was up to those eight to play the game without any help from any prompters.

One thing about the cards and the rambling, or wherever else you were, was that you had to be at home in time for the Rosary, that is unless it had been said before you left. If the Rosary had to be said after the card game was over the players were told to finish the game good and fast, that it was time to hit the hay. In our house the Rosary was always said between ten and eleven o'clock. When we had the house to ourselves my father went down on his knees and everybody else did the same. My mother always started the Rosary and my father

jump in over the fence and down to the bottom of the nearest field. But now young people give impudence and cheek to priests. Of course you would recognise a priest at that time, but a priest might be at a dance nowadays and you would never take him to be a priest because he wouldn't be dressed like one.

They say that a dumb priest never gets his dues, and that is true. They say too that money marks the end of the Gospel. But priests weren't very flush with money because they had no hope of getting what the poor people didn't have. The parish priest got the Christmas collection and that wasn't a whole lot. If I am not greatly mistaken those who owned cows were assessed at a shilling a cow. I do know that when I was young no farmer in the parish had twenty cows, nor fifteen nor maybe even ten. All the curate got was the collection which we called 'oats money' and that was little or nothing. Because he had a horse he needed oats and of course he didn't get oats for nothing. Every priest now has a car. That requires another type of 'oats' which is dear nowadays.

5
'... EXCEPT MY CHILD'

I was always a great one for burying the dead and I still am. It is not because of my faith or holiness, although our catechism told us that it was one of the works of mercy. Maybe it was something I inherited because I had relatives, aunts and uncles and especially my father himself, who loved to go burying the dead. Then again maybe in my cuteness I was doing it to avoid work. In any case as soon as I heard that somebody was being buried I had a great excuse to get away from the house. If there was something to be done at home, something that I dreaded, I would say, 'I'm going to the funeral today'.

Often on the day of a funeral I meet someone I haven't met for quite a while and he might give me a dig saying: 'You're here again!'

I answer politely that I am. Then he says: 'If you had anything to do you would have stayed at home.'

One day – I was hardly twelve years old at the time – I heard there was to be a funeral in Dunurlin. That is my own burial-ground because my family are buried there and I presume that I too will go there, with God's help. Anyhow I went to the funeral. There were no motor-cars there as there are at funerals nowadays, nothing only horses and carts. We all stood around the graveyard. The person to be buried was buried, a young girl. The earth was shovelled in. The last sod was put in place, and a decade of the Rosary was said. If I live to be a hundred I'll never forget the words the girl's mother uttered as we left the churchyard: 'Everyone is going home except my child'.

That is over half a century ago. I don't know why those words are still so clear in my head but that was probably the first funeral I attended. Ever since when a local person or even someone a long way away dies I love going to bury them if I have any means of getting there.

Where death and wakes are concerned the neighbours at

34

that time were much more charitable than they are nowadays. Maybe they are still charitable but do not need to show it because customs have changed. If I died tomorrow morning I would be whisked off down to Dingle and I suppose that is where I would be washed and cleaned, and maybe I might need it! But long ago the corpse was always kept at home. If he died in the evening he was kept in the house that night and all the following day and the night after that again and then he was removed east to Dunurlin or maybe west to Dunquin, or wherever his bones were destined to be laid at the end of his days.

When he died his corpse was laid out. If his death was expected they might already have the habit in the house. If not it was just a matter of going to Dingle and bringing home the habit. Two tables were needed to lay him out because one would be too short. That meant going to the neighbour's house for the second one. The two tables were placed end to end and the corpse laid down on them. He was ready to be waked then and that was when the keening and the crying started. The keening women entered in twos or threes and the minute they saw the corpse laid out on the table they went up to it. Then they started crying and raising and lowering their voices and raising and lowering their bodies.

'Well, isn't he nice!' they would say. 'He looks far and away better today than he did a fortnight ago.'

Such praise as the person got then, even if he was the devil himself or had the makings of a devil! But a lot of it was just roguery and hypocrisy because I was old enough and crabbed enough then to notice that very often there were no tears on those women's faces, nothing only the crying and the praise, the sorrow and the heartbreak caused by his death, and what would they do without him. Talk about praise! You would never believe it unless you heard them. The day of your wedding or the day of your wake, they say, are the only two days of your life that you receive praise, whether you are good or bad.

I saw it for myself. I didn't understand it then as well as I do now. The last wake I attended and at which the corpse was keened took place not far from here and my feeling about it is praise be to God forever that the keening was done away with. We are better off without it. In those days they used to keen everyone, even if he was a hundred and fifty years old. I know of one fellow who was very near the hundred and I remember that he was keened just as would a person of only twenty. Nowadays if people wanted to cry twenty-one times over they wouldn't get a chance to do so because as soon as ever the person dies – he mightn't even be dead or cold at all – he is rushed into Dingle and waked there. And he isn't really waked at all because the corpse is on its own the whole day until evening when it is removed to its own church, whether that be east, west, north or south.

The world and his mother used to come to the wakehouse. Everybody was given food and drink and tobacco. White pipes were supplied too with two or maybe three people covered in sweat cutting tobacco, filling the pipes and putting them on coolers on the fences outside the house. According as each person arrived the first thing he or she did – the women also smoked tobacco, something you don't see nowadays – was to put a pipe in their mouth and, whether they were in earnest or not, they prayed for the dead person. Snuff was also provided, with two or three people in charge of it. It was put out on plates and saucers and passed all around the house.

If the family was in any way well off they would have a barrel of porter, and those who drank would keep their eye on the barrel just like hundreds or maybe thousands of flies would keep their eyes on a stinking piece of meat especially in the middle of summer. People who had travelled ten or twenty miles or who were connected with or related to the dead person were called to one side into a room where the hard drop was kept. But, whether the drop was hard or soft, if it was at all plentiful it didn't take long to go to their heads. At two, three or four o'clock in the morning they longed for nothing more than to be allowed to sing a song, and that is why I believe that their tears were only crocodile tears. They were crying coming in and singing before going home.

On the day of the funeral the corpse was placed in the

coffin and the lid was put on. Then it was brought out of the house and placed on two chairs. Every stitch of clothing on the bed had to be folded up and thrown in under the bed. I never found out the origin of that custom and I don't suppose I ever will. What makes me laugh, and it isn't so long since it last happened, is that the two chairs had to be knocked over when the coffin was raised up to be shouldered. If that wasn't done it was believed – and it was a strange belief – that the deceased person's soul would remain in purgatory until the two chairs were put standing on their legs again. Then when the funeral left the house a group of women – you would swear that they were being paid like the keening women – would start crying as they moved down the road or up the road and you could hear them still wailing a half-mile away.

The men took turns at carrying the coffin. When they came to a crossroads – I mean a real crossroads, not a boreen used by animals or horses, but one like Ballyferriter Crossroads, say – the coffin had to be placed on the ground and the four men carrying it would put their boots under it. The idea behind that was so that they could get a grip on the coffin when putting it up on their shoulders again. The people on horseback then stopped. So did everybody else. They took off their caps – there were very few hats in those days – and said a prayer for the dead. There was a grassy triangle in the centre of Sheana-cnuck Crossroads, east of Ballyferriter, that is until the County Council came and took it away. That was known as 'the triangle of the dead' where the coffin was placed on the ground while the prayer was being said.

One day I was at a funeral together with a friend of mine. We had two bicycles but left them at the wakehouse. The corpse was brought out. There weren't many people present and so we ourselves and two others had to go under the coffin. Myself and my friend were the same height and, upon my word, only that we were there and were young and strong I don't think it would have been possible to bring it up the hill where we brought it. After burying the dead man we had to walk back to the wakehouse and get our bicycles and go home. That was all there was to it.

I know of another person who had to be carried from Ballyferriter Church to Dunquin. That is quite a long journey, a good five miles, and one man was too tall and too hefty for the men around him with the result that his shoulder was skinned for four months after the day of the funeral. What baffles me is why they didn't put the corpse into a horse-cart instead of carrying it on their shoulders.

6
TRAINS AND TRAINING

Ever since I was in petticoats if you were to ask me 'What will you be when you grow up, Tomás?' my answer would have been that I would be a priest. God knows it would be a poor lookout for the Church if she had to depend on me as a priest. Still I was in earnest about it even up to the time I became a man.

There were two ladies from Cork who had a summer house in Graigue, Mary and Annie MacSwiney, sisters of Terence who had died on hunger-strike in London some years before that. I got to know themselves and their friend Sinéad Ní Bhriain, and many is the message I brought them from Ballyferriter. They were very friendly with me and by degrees I shared my secret with Mary, the older sister of the two. The secret was that I was very keen on becoming a priest.

I used to teach Mary Irish and in return she tried to teach me Latin. I don't know if she had any money, and it didn't matter whether she had or not as long as she helped me with the Latin at which I was very weak, and which was so necessary for me if it was the will of God that I should become a priest some fine day. But now and again if I didn't use the correct teaching method Mary would get very cross and say impatiently: 'I want the construction!' But I didn't have the foggiest notion what the construction meant.

Mary promised that she would get me a place in some college or other and she kept that promise – may she reap her reward for it – when I was in or about twenty years old and still had the same desire to be a priest. One day in September I left Graigue for the first time and set out for the Sacred Heart College for priests in Ballinafad, County Mayo. That college was owned by the African Missionaries. Another chap, Seán de Brún from Gallaras, was with me going there.

We had to spend the first night in Limerick, myself and Seán, and another young man from Ballineanaig, Seán Ó Súilleabháin, who was a school teacher near Limerick City. Ó Súil-leabháin, God rest him, was our guide. Ronan's Hotel was the name of the place where we stayed, and the old lady who owned it was very polite indeed, very nice and gentle. She provided us with everything we needed. I suppose she was called to her eternal reward long ago. The three of us were in one room. It had two beds. Myself and De Brún slept in one and Ó Súilleabháin had a single bed.

The two of them went out walking for a while and I was left in the room on my own. I stretched myself on the bed, and I don't know if it was panic or loneliness that came over me or whether I fell asleep and had a nightmare, but anyhow I jumped out of bed and ran down the stairs looking for my man De Brún. The landlady met me at the bottom of the stairs and asked my why was I so frightened. I told her my problem, that there was something in the room that wasn't to my liking. She went back upstairs with me and we searched but there was nothing there but my shadow.

The other two came back after their walk. I told them my story – a ridiculous one, whatever put it into my body or my head – that the devil was under the bed and was trying to stop me from going for the priesthood. I was for all the world like the Curé d'Ars, the French saint of whom it is said that the devil burned his bed. But I can't say if I had already heard that story when the devil tried to kill me or burn me in my bed while I was on my way to do what was best for me.

It seems that the president of the College in Ballinafad knew Mary MacSwiney of old. The first evening I arrived there he came looking for me and gave me a most hearty welcome. He knew very well that Mary was responsible for my being there. His name was Fr McNamara from Cork City, a fine man if ever there was, pleasant and kind.

For a grown man life there was very strange compared to the life I had left behind in Graigue. I observed only one rule in Graigue and that was to come and go as I felt like it. Maybe I was full of high spirits then unlike the days when I was a small boy going to Ballyferriter School. I had all I wanted to eat, and on the other hand maybe I hadn't. No matter, I survived. But I found the life in the College strange. Everything was hard, everything was different. What a change, going to bed in broad daylight at the end of summer or the beginning of autumn instead of going out playing football. That is what really killed me. I wasn't the only one who complained. Everybody else complained too although the big majority of the lads were much younger than myself. I was four years older than some of them and perhaps five years older than others.

The priests themselves were hard. We thought they were unnatural in the way they treated us. It was just a case of 'beckon and come!' You got no satisfaction if you told them you were short of this or of that. Once a week we went on a big long walk so many miles from the College, a priest ahead of us and a priest behind in case we might rob or steal or swipe something, though every single one of us, I felt, was deadly serious about becoming a priest. Why were they afraid to let us out on our own? Myself and Seán de Brún and another chap named Cunningham, the three tallest, were always in front of the group with the other poor unfortunates trailing along behind, thirty-three all told. But as for myself I feel I wasn't ready in many ways to take up the great challenge of becoming a priest.

I didn't have enough clothes due to the scarcity of money. Before I ever left Graigue a priest gave me a list of things that I would need to bring with me to the college. I remember that a heavy overcoat was very necessary to protect me from the cold that comes in County Mayo during the winter – and take it from me it does get cold there – and also a hat or a small peaked cap like a jockey would have, only that it had to be black. Everything was black except your shirt which was bright, and your heart, if that too was bright. But I had neither an overcoat nor a hat nor a cap, and neither myself nor anybody belonging to me had the money to buy them. Only for the kindness of two lads from the north who were there with me and had more than enough and shared with me I would have been a long time without a coat.

We were allowed home for Christmas and of course I travelled on the Dingle train west from Tralee. It was worth being on that same train at Christmas time when the world and his mother came home from England and from every part of Ireland, young people and old. The hearts of the old were just as light and as young as the hearts of the young because there was nothing to compare with coming home for Christmas. That was the loveliest custom we ever had and thank God we still have it.

Talking about the train, there will never again be one like it and God forbid that there should. When the tide came in around Blennerville after a heavy fall of rain there wasn't a hope that the train could go any farther and it would have to stop in the middle of the flood. There was nothing to do then but pull up your legs, stretch out or sit on your haunches on the seat and wait for the tide to go out. Then when the tide went out the water subsided and the train would set out for home. That was the sprightly train! Thirty miles from Tralee to Dingle and it used to take it a full three hours to do the journey!

If you were at Dingle Station as the train was on its way from the east you could hear the whistle while it was still in Lispole five miles or so away. 'Here it comes!' you would say. Such clatter and noise and smoke out of it as it came into the station! The world and his mother would be waiting for it and you couldn't imagine the chattering and talk with most of the people speaking in Irish.

The greatest confusion of all was on the journey from Dingle to Tralee, especially from Annascaul east. There was nothing as amusing as watching the women trying to hoosh hens and geese and ducks and turkeys into the train. Some of them would have anything from a chicken to a turkey-cock under their arms and more would have a big basket of eggs to sell in Tralee and make a few pence so that they could bring home a bite of food that evening.

I remember one day there was a football match in Tralee and I cycled there. Myself and the train left Dingle together and I was in Tralee before it! That is no lie because there are people still alive who were on the train and saw me. Going up the hill at Glannagalt is where I beat it. It would remind you of an old cow because it was always panting trying to get to the top of the hill. It ran beside the road for most of the way but once in a while it would take the notion to cross the road from right to left or from left to right, with no warning whatsoever to anyone coming towards it or behind it.

The Dingle train caused its own share of destruction in its day. Once it went off the rails altogether near Camp and killed a lot of pigs. On another occasion it was going downhill somewhere around Glannagalt and came upon a fine donkey that wasn't taking care of himself. When he heard the noise and commotion making for him didn't the devil tempt him to cross the railway track! I suppose it was the smoke that smothered him. In any case he got a wallop. The train had to stop, naturally. Three or four men got out and pulled the donkey out from under the front wheel, but I am afraid he was never again tackled under a cart because within half a minute he was as dead as a doornail.

It must be said, however, that the train was convenient for people because at that time there were no motor-cars going to Tralee except once in a while, if at all. The Dingle train was later done away with and buses put in its place, and that was the first of the great changes that have taken place in this area since I was a young fellow.

Anyhow when I was coming near the house on that first visit home for Christmas I remember meeting a great friend of mine from Clogher on the road in the dusk. When I saluted him he recognised my voice, yet he thought I looked strange. I was wearing a black hat, a black suit, a black tie and a white shirt. I was rigged out in great style. Instead of speaking and saluting me he walked around me to look at me right and left.

'It is never you!' he said to me.

'It is,' I said.

'Are you a priest?' he said.

'I will be soon,' I said.

This is what he said to somebody who met him on the road the following day: 'Didn't I meet Tomás last night! He had come home and his clothes were so black and his manner so changed, so gentle and so nice and so holy, that I was going to ask him to give me absolution. And I hope it won't be long until he does.'

7
DOWN – AND OUT!

When I went in home my father was there to welcome me and the lamp was lighting. When he saw me in my black clothes he was so proud that in his innocence the first thing he said was: 'How long more will it be until you are a priest?' When he saw my appearance and the collar round my neck he thought it was only a matter of turning the collar back and giving him my blessing. A long wait on weak legs! Everyone was happy and I got a great welcome. They made a drop of tea and then a woman from the townland, Small Cáit, the Lord have mercy on her soul, walked in. Cáit had a tongue as fluent as anyone I ever heard and had her own way of saying things. She was no stammerer but a gifted speaker and I often wonder since what was wrong with me that I didn't take down a lot of her sayings. I would have got them from her with a heart and a half.

'Yerrah, a thousand welcomes, Tomáisín,' she said. 'You're looking great altogether.'

'I am, Cáit, thank you,' I said.

I suppose I had changed a little. I had been away for a couple of months and experienced that place in Mayo. Another field, other grass, other food and other people.

'Why wouldn't he be looking great?' my father said. 'Isn't he in a college for priests?'

'Wouldn't you shut your mouth, you brat?' says she. 'How well you didn't go to be a priest yourself!'

They got stuck in one another but it was all in fun and jest.

I went back to Ballinafad after Christmas sad and broken-hearted because I wasn't at all satisfied there with the way things were going.

As for games we played football every day except when the weather was too wet. Even if there was frost and snow on the ground we had to go out playing in our short little togs, but we never minded the weather once the game started. We never had a referee, just the priest walking up and down the sideline

45

as he read his Office. We hadn't enough players to have a worthwhile match because some of them knew nothing at all about football. They didn't even know how to catch the ball.

This particular day when the ground was covered with snow some sort of a row broke out between myself and a chap named Welby from Tuam. I flattened him with a belt of a fist. As luck would have it just at that moment the priest took his two eyes off the book to look at the game. Didn't he spot me! He called me over and he didn't call me Tomás.

'Kennedy, come here!' he said.

I went over to him. What else could I do? I was like a little mouse facing a cat. I knew I was in for some sort of punishment. That was the rule. All he said was: 'Get down there now on your two knees.' I did so, in the snow. God above, when I think of it now, I would have been a damned sight better off then, I imagine, if I had said to him: 'Go to blazes, Father! I'm going home to Graigue', and then gone in, put on my clothes and headed off home, because I thought it odd that I, a grown man, should be on my knees in the middle of a field covered with snow. Those rules didn't suit me because I wasn't prepared to put up with them.

There was one subject I didn't do in the College, because I wasn't obliged to, and that was Irish. I was learning Latin instead because I was very weak altogether at it. I had picked up a few words of Latin at school in Dingle – two months I think I spent there – before I ever went to Ballinafad. I found it very hard. It took me, I suppose, a full six months to learn the 'Our Father who art in heaven' by heart in Latin, and as for answering Mass I imagine it took me a year and still I hadn't mastered it. But nowadays I pretend I have Latin, especially when I am talking to people who don't know a word of it. In the presence of people who do know it I keep my mouth shut.

Bad and all as things were, and they were bad enough for anything, I spent the full year in the College as I was supposed to. Then June came and we got our summer holidays. When leaving we had been given to understand that we were to attend another college the following September, but I had finished with Ballinafad forever because I never since laid eyes on the place.

Three months' holidays in Graigue! I could write twenty-one books about that alone, even if I wrote about nothing else but the pleasure and the enjoyment that was to be got from being on holidays there. By the way we used to get fine summers in those days. You would get a full week or a fortnight or maybe a month of sunshine and heat without a break. It is a far different story nowadays.

I didn't do much work at home although I used to give it a try now and again, but I was convinced that work was something fit only for horses or donkeys. That was how I always felt about it. I wondered why my poor father killed himself working day after day, but then that is how he wanted it. Yet he had nothing to show for his work, nor had many others either. That was why I had a bicycle instead of a shovel.

The days were passing by. After the summer holidays myself and my friend Seán de Brún went to the African Missions' College in Wilton in Cork City. The two of us were attached to each other from the beginning. We have been friends ever since and will be until the day death comes between us. Seán is a priest out in Africa this long time.

When we got to Cork we found out from a busman where Wilton College was. We arrived there and it looked as if there wasn't a living soul under the roof of the house. We thought that we would be given a really great welcome, especially because they were expecting us, but it was not to be. There wasn't a sinner there to meet us. The house was fairly large and there was a chapel beside it. We started looking around and walking up and down east and west in front of the big house in the hope that someone would notice us and come out, so we thought, to welcome us, but no one came. The first inkling we got that there was someone alive there was when we saw four or five boys like ourselves coming towards us. They had just arrived. We introduced ourselves to one another. Finally we met a priest and he told us what to do, bring our bags up to the dormitory and go for a bite to eat about six or seven o'clock in the evening, our first meal in the place.

Believe you me there wasn't much difference between life

in Cork and life in County Mayo because the rules in both places were similar. Myself and Seán were different from all the other students because we were native speakers of Irish. Yet we weren't given any greater welcome than anybody else. They didn't take any great notice of us when speaking in Irish to one another. Our Irish teacher, who was a priest, was kind of jealous of us, and now when I think back on his antics I realise it. We were allowed to stay in the class but that teacher never asked us any questions because he knew that we could teach him the language.

There was another priest there, a very small little man, and whatever notion I took I went into the confession box to him one day. I don't know if I was in the state of sin at that time. I have a lazy man's load of sins on me now, though. Anyhow, just as I used to do in Ballyferriter before I ever went away, I said to him in Irish: 'Bless me Father, for I have sinned,' but the first thing he said to me, and he was very nice about it, was: 'My dear child, I don't know your language. Go elsewhere'.

I just came out of the box and asked somebody or other if there was any priest there with a smattering of my own language. I was told there was so I went into him and told him my story, but I guarantee you that his Irish was poor enough. Whether he understood me or not he gave me absolution. That priest was the President of the College.

The President of Ballinafad was a fine type but the President of Wilton didn't have the same sort of mentality at all. He was a grumpy-looking fellow who never smiled. He did his job and that was all.

There was another priest – I hear that he is still alive – who took special notice of me. He certainly did. I don't know what he had against me but when he came into the class the first thing I always had to do was to stand up, leave my seat, go back a certain distance and stay there on my own. At that time there was a Kerry footballer known as 'The Gallery Player'. That is the nickname which this priest gave me, and he would say in English: 'Will ye look back at the Gallery Player?' The whole class would turn around and look back, but they didn't laugh at me or mock me. In fact they had pity for me.

I was getting on fine, I thought. I was as good as anyone else, keeping up with the class, sleeping, eating, and playing when the weather was suitable. They weren't as strict here about football as they were in County Mayo. It was a pity that we weren't allowed outside the gate as they are now to play an outside team, young or old it didn't matter. We had a great team because we had up to seventy players altogether, but what good was that?

The day came in the middle of June when we were due to get our holidays. The rule about travelling was that you had to go to the President's room, get your ticket to wherever you were going and pay for it. As you would expect myself and Seán were going to Dingle. Before the President handed me my ticket, or at least before I parted with the money, he said something that startled me. He told me that I would not be returning there next term.

I didn't say a word, I just grabbed the ticket from him and went off. I looked neither right nor left at the lads who were outside waiting for their turn to go in, but I headed for the Chapel and talked really seriously with the God of Glory. I told him my story and asked him to help me. Maybe he did. We must wait and see, but it has always been said that he never refused anyone help who asked for it in the proper manner.

On the following day I came home to Graigue very depressed. I was so fed up with life that I would have preferred to be dead. A bush had been placed before me in the gap and what really killed me was that they never gave me any idea as to what they had against me. I thought I was as humble and well-behaved and mannerly as any lad there, and most eager to be a priest.

That was the year 1936. During the summer I wrote a letter to the Mill Hill Fathers in Freshford, County Kilkenny. I told them what had happened, that I had spent a couple of years with the African Missionaries, that I had failed but didn't know why, and that I was still as keen as ever to become a priest. A week passed and a month passed and still I heard nothing from them until this particular day that I went to the strand with a horse and cart for a load of sand. When I arrived home there was a small car at the bottom of the boreen on the main road, or the King's Road as we used to call it. I didn't take any great notice of it though I had an idea that the owner was in our house.

As I was coming near the house my mother appeared at the door. 'Untackle the horse fast,' she said. 'There's a priest here who wants to talk to you.'

I went in. The priest, a young fair-haired man, was sitting at the top of the table. I remember him clearly. He had no Irish but you may be sure that I had enough English. My mother went out. We got down to business and the priest questioned me as to my situation and what had caused me to leave Wilton. I told him the truth. I didn't twist the story in any way. He was talking about this and that until he came to the question that amazed me, had I been vaccinated against smallpox! Before I answered him upon my soul I thought to myself, what a strange question! What had the priesthood to do with my being vaccinated against smallpox or not? Couldn't you anoint a person without being vaccinated?

'I haven't,' I said, telling him the truth because I hadn't.

He asked me then if my father could afford to pay ten pounds a year for me in college. I told him that I didn't think he could, and I was right, because it would have been hard for the likes of my father to come by that kind of money in those days. The priest reduced the figure then. 'Do you think your father could pay five pounds a year?' he said.

I gave the same answer to that question.

'All right, my child,' he said. A child he called me though I was a big hefty man!

'I'm afraid I can't accept you,' he said, and he stood up, shook hands with me and went off out. I have never seen him since nor have I heard any more of him.

I said to myself then that I would try the Salesians in Pallaskenry in County Limerick. I cycled the forty miles to Tralee on an old bicycle and stayed the night there with my brother Micheál. He wasn't married at that time. The following day I got a lift in a van belonging to the *Cork Examiner* that was going to Limerick. The driver dropped me at a certain crossroads. I enquired where the College was and found it. I knocked on the door. Somebody or other answered, and I said I wanted to speak to a priest. A priest came out and I told him my story.

'Come in,' he said.

He brought me into a big room. We talked for a little while.

'I'm prepared to accept you,' he said, 'on condition that you do this much for me.'

The task he gave me, or if you like, the obstacle he put in my way, was to open a book, read a certain page inside in the middle of it and learn it by heart while he himself was out. Ten minutes he gave me to do it. He went out and shut the door behind him. I took a look at the book and read the page. Then I said to myself: 'There's not a hope in hell that I'll be able to learn this off by heart in ten minutes.' That was all there was to it. I didn't even try. The priest came back. He asked me if I had succeeded and I gave him an honest answer and I told him I hadn't, as indeed was the case.

I was beaten again, and that was the last attempt I made to become a priest. Maybe it was the will of God because I suppose I wasn't cut out for it.

Whenever I am on my own, and unfortunately I often am, I start thinking. I am afraid that many a time instead of thinking about God I look back instead on the days of my youth and on the great efforts I feel I made to do what my heart was set on, although I knew for certain by then that I had failed completely. It was then the thought struck me that the worst thing that could ever happen to a person is to give him a place of honour on the top of a tree and then cut down the tree, because that person falls to the ground. I had taken the first fall. There were more falls ahead of me.

A person must have some aim and purpose in life. We are told that when we were created a certain road was laid out before us. I believe that. We are also told that there are certain things we must do other than evil. What purpose had I up to now in coming into the world at all, or what mark have I left on the world, if it was God's will to call me tomorrow morning? I never did anything worthwhile because I didn't get the schooling I needed. A good start is half the battle. I got a good start sure enough but before half the work had been completed my schooling was over because I didn't have the means to pay for it.

I am not crying or moaning when I say that I didn't get a fair crack of the whip, and not only myself but thousands of others as well, people who were a lot more intelligent than I was. There were fellows ahead of me, in the same class and behind me in school who would now be famous if only their parents could afford the money to pay for their schooling. There are young people in schools today, they are even in colleges today, who are as stupid as an old donkey. They have been pushed in there because there are people behind them who have what is needed to put them there. I am not saying that because of any desire for money. I never had any desire for it. It is not that I wouldn't have loved to have as much as I needed. I am afraid that I never had that much, or if I had I didn't hold on too long to it, and I hope that I won't leave any wealth after me the day I die.

There was a nun I knew who tried right go wrong to persuade me that I would do much more for God by not becoming a priest at all but by remaining a layman, which I had to do in any case. But I told her that I didn't agree with her and I would say the very same to her today only that she has gone to her eternal reward. She said that a good father is better than a bad priest, and that is true. I can't be called a good priest or a bad one because the collar was never turned around on my neck, and, as for being a father, no one can say that I was a good father or a bad one because I never paid any attention to the cackling of women.

8

AN BOTHÁN DUBH

Not long after I returned home from Wilton my life took another turn with the coming of An tAthair Tadhg Ó Murchú to Graigue. An tAthair Tadhg was from Killaminogue near Innishannon in County Cork, and was teaching in Farranferris Seminary in Cork City. He was only six months a priest when he came to Graigue for the first time between the two Christmases in 1935–6. He was just another priest, yet he stood out above all the other priests because of his zeal and his loyalty.

I met him myself the second day after he came. He was looking for a field or a bit of a field for the coming summer so that he could bring a group of boys from the Seminary to Graigue to improve whatever Irish he himself had taught them.

I introduced him to my father because I knew very well that my father would never refuse him. Meagre and all as my father's means were he gave a thousand welcomes to the priest because all during his life he had great regard and respect for priests, and his words were: 'You'll get the best field I have for nothing'. Of course the holy priest wasn't looking for it for nothing. Whatever arrangements required to be made were made and there was no solicitor present nor any need of one.

An tAthair Tadhg came on holidays the following July with a dozen or so students and a bell-tent they had got on loan from the army. They put up their tent in a field known as Gerard's Lower Field below the road. It was their misfortune that during their first night there they were hit by wind and rain coming east from the Candle Stone. The centre pole was broken, the tent fell down on top of them and they had to head for our house for shelter at the dead of night.

They were taken care of. A blazing fire was put down. Their clothes were dried. A drop of tea was made. That is how the weather welcomed An tAthair Tadhg. The following day brought a different story. The sun came out again and gave him a real welcome. The tent was repaired and they stayed three weeks. That was how An tAthair Tadhg started in Graigue.

The following year, 1937, his clutch had increased somewhat, and they built An Bothán Dubh or Black Hut at the back of our house. Timber and nails were the only materials used. Still and all it lasted. It is still there. Because I had nothing to do during the summer other than cavorting around the place I became very friendly and very involved with them. As well as that An tAthair Tadhg was very anxious that I should help his boys with Irish since they were so keen to learn it. The Bothán Dubh did the world of good. Some fine boys came there who are grown men this long time and no matter where you travelled in this great big world today there is a good chance that you might meet someone who was in the Bothán Dubh at some stage and would speak Irish to you the same as he did when he was in Graigue.

They were coming and going for six weeks every year until 1955 when the big hostel, An Brú, was built, and from that day on the spirit began to wane. The enthusiasm declined when the Bothán Dubh ceased to be used and as well as that since the warrior himself, An tAthair Tadhg, died in 1971 no one came in his place who could possibly fill his shoes. As someone said after his death: 'He was a small man, and yet he was a giant'.

He had done wonderful work and although he didn't achieve a great deal by way of literature or writing he made a lasting impact.

In the beginning of autumn 1937 An tAthair Tadhg invited me to spend a while with him in his parents' home in Killaminogue. I gladly took up the invitation because I was at a loose end and didn't care as long as I had somewhere to go. I spent a fortnight there and served his Mass every morning.

The day came for him to go back teaching in Farranferris. That was the very day I got the notion to come home to Graigue. I travelled with him into Cork City. Before we parted he handed me a half-sovereign so that I could go home in style, in other words by train to Dingle. That was a lot of money in those days. Half of it would take me to Graigue. But, I am afraid, I put the money into my pocket and took to the road home on foot. I hadn't gone very far when I got a lift but the driver dropped me at Dripsey about twelve miles west of Cork. The sun was setting and was very low in the sky by this time. What should I do, continue on walking or look for lodgings or a hayshed?

I saw five or six lads playing pitch-and-toss on the side of the road a little bit away from me and I asked them shyly if there was any house where a fellow might get lodgings for the night. I made no mention of money. They had a little chat amongst themselves and then one of them turned to me and said: 'I know where there's someone who would gladly welcome you.'

He pointed out the house. He didn't say anything about why I might be needed, and I didn't care. All I wanted was to be indoors from the night sky. I got to the house, knocked on the door and was told to come in, in English as you might expect. I went in. There was a man on his own inside and I said to him: 'It is like this. I'd love if you could let me stay the night.'

'You're very welcome,' he said.

My heart rose. I soon found out why I was so welcome. His wife had given birth to a child that morning and she was still in her childbed down in the room at the bottom of the house, and he wanted to have someone who would stay up with him. I agreed.

We started chatting. I found out he was a tailor, a nice man. Neither of us slept a wink during the night, nothing but tea and more tea. The child bawled from time to time and so did the woman. They had every second turn at it and he himself was kept busy running up and down to the room. I was old enough to understand the predicament of the person in the bed. Still and all I was of no help to them. I did nothing but sit by the fire and talk to himself. I wasn't even smoking then not to mind drinking. Yet I suppose I did some good because I kept him company.

Anyhow shortly after the morning dawned I told him I was going to hit the road. He was quite satisfied. He put his hand in his pocket and handed me a shilling. I now had eleven shillings setting out on the road to Dingle. I thought I was rich. Off I went. When I got as far as Coachford another few miles to the west I called into the parish priest for a drop of tea.

The housekeeper answered the knock on the door. She called out the priest. Now I didn't have the look of a beggar. Maybe if I had I might be welcome, but I didn't at all like the scowl that man put on his face. He told me good and fast to be off, which I did. It was no time for delaying or talking.

I got a lift from there into Macroom where I had the misfortune to go into the Garda Barracks of all places still looking for a drop of tea. I knew that they weren't likely to make a collection for me. The man in charge there was a Kerryman. I suppose he has gone to his eternal reward by now. It is time for him because he was no child then, and I promise you he wasn't up to much, the ruffian. All I said to him was that I would love a drop of tea. He asked me a thousand questions.

When he found out who I was and how things were with me, a big able-bodied young man, he said: 'What the devil is wrong with you that you don't join the army and be a man?'

I was sorry I called in there at all. I wasn't a bit thankful to my legs for having brought me there. I was left with no choice but to go out and hit the road again. I got another lift as far as Killarney. I had to pay a shilling there for a drop of tea. It broke my heart to part with it, not because of any love for money but because I thought I would bring home intact the eleven shillings I had got in Cork.

I stayed in Tralee with my brother Micheál that night. Who should give me a lift to Ballyferriter the next day but my own parish priest, An tAthair Tomás Ó Muircheartaigh! You could never imagine such fun as we had, I telling him about my adventures, especially about the newborn child, and he with his mouth wide open back to his ears listening to me. He nearly hit the fence a couple of times because that was just like what he would do on hearing a funny story. I reached home at long last very pleased with myself. As the old saying goes: 'Bad and all as the old shack is the home is the place to be.'

I was thinking all the time of what the old sergeant in Macroom had said about joining the army. The thought was soon translated into action.

9
OFF TO DUBLIN

I left Graigue one day in the summer of the year 1936, and probably nobody except my own family knew where I was going. Outside Ballyferriter I met a friend of mine, Breandán Ó hUallacháin, who many years later was destined to become aide-de-camp to President De Valera. He has gone to his eternal reward since, God be good to him.

'Where are you going?' he said. 'To Dingle?'

'Maybe you won't believe me,' I said. 'I'm on my way to Dublin.'

'You're on your way to Dublin on that thing!' he said, referring to my bicycle. 'I wouldn't go to Dingle on it.'

'Well, maybe not, but I'm going to Dublin on it anyhow,' I answered, saying goodbye to him, but it was clear that he didn't believe me.

It was latish by the time I left Ballyferriter. Three shillings was all I had in my pocket. I was aiming to get as far as Kilmeedy in County Limerick nearly ninety miles away. There was a schoolfriend of mine living there and I knew that he would have a welcome for me. He is a priest in America this long time. I was cycling away at full tilt but the night began to fall while I was still nowhere near Kilmeedy. I said to myself that I would have to set about getting some lodgings somewhere, even if only by the side of a fence or in a hayshed. I tried a couple of houses but was refused. Upon my soul it reminded me of nothing but the night Our Saviour, praise be to him forever, came into the world, when neither St Joseph nor the Blessed Virgin was taken into the inn because they were too poor and so they had to go in amongst the sheep.

Coming up to eleven o'clock I tried another house outside Abbeyfeale. It was a big long thatched house and had all the signs of food and wealth but I hadn't tried it yet. I knocked on the door. A major of a woman came out, and still somehow or other she wasn't a major, as I soon found out.

'What is troubling you?' said she in English.

'It is like this, my good woman,' I said. 'I'm on my way to Dublin, and I would love to get lodgings for the night, if you could manage it.'

'Isn't there a town near you,' she said, 'and hotels there?'

'There is,' I said, drawing in my horns, 'but I haven't got a whole lot in my pocket.'

Then she asked what I thought was the silliest and the queerest question anyone could ask another.

'Are you Catholic?' she said to me.

'Of course I am,' I said, 'and all belonging to me.'

'Are you sure you're a Catholic?'

'Why wouldn't I be sure?' I said.

'Have you any proof?' she said.

'I have,' said I, putting my hand in my pocket and showing her my Rosary beads.

She took my word for it. She didn't give me anything to eat but took me upstairs to a room with a double bed and told me I could stretch in it. But, oh God of Graces, as bad luck would have it who should come up after me but the servant boy! It was his bed. He went on the inside and I went on the outside. I didn't care as long as I was indoors from the night sky. I fell asleep and woke, I fell asleep and woke, but one thing I do know, and that is that the poor fellow on the inside didn't sleep a wink for fear that I might have a knife or a gun and go for his throat in the hope that he might have money. He had one eye open and one eye closed just like a hare has when asleep. I knew how he felt though.

I set off again the next morning with a big long day ahead of me. I felt a bit more hopeful because I was making for Kilmeedy and knew that it wasn't very far away. I spent two days and two nights there and I could easily have spent a month there because I was welcome, but that was not what I had in mind. I wanted to see the big city of Dublin for the first time.

I got to Limerick City in no time. Down I went through the middle of O'Connell Street. I had no notion of buying this or that. I just looked right and left. I felt like going into a couple of shops but if I did I would have had two or three assistants coming up to me to find out what I wanted to buy, and I knew well how much I had in my pocket. I never stopped until I got to the Tipperary border. I can't exactly say which side of the border I was on when the chain of the bicycle broke, and what was I to do then? Nothing but look round at the back wheel. Now where would you be going without a chain on your bicycle? Just then the train from Limerick came along very near the road on its way to Dublin. Oh God of Bright Glory! That really broke my heart. There I was unable to stir or even raise my hand to stop the train because if I did I would have been arrested.

Thank God the world was always full of fine people and always will be. I called into a house with the chain in my hand. There was a young chap inside.

'It is like this,' I said, 'I'm going to Dublin and my chain is broken.'

He replied in English. It didn't take him very long at all to fix the chain. He put the bicycle in working order and I got a drop of tea from his mother. I was ready for the road again.

I had a fair idea of the road as any tramp would need to have to do his job properly, so I thought of the Cistercian Monastery near Roscrea. I headed straight for it and it didn't take me very long to get there. I went in. I met a priest. I told him my situation.

'Oh, that's what we are here for,' he said. 'You're welcome, and you can stay as long as you like.'

All I wanted was one night. Sure enough I was given a meal. What upset me most, though, and I still think of it, was that I don't think I left very much under the saucer when I was going away next morning, simply because I didn't have it.

I left the Monastery and went as far as County Laois. I was very well able to make my way around. Outside Portlaoise there lived a chap named Scully who had been in school with me in Wilton. I found the house. His people just couldn't do enough for me and invited me to stay a day, two days, three days or a week if I wished. But that wasn't what I had in mind. I told them that I was going to Dublin but that I didn't know the city at all. What did two of the lads in the house do but draw out a map that would guide me into the city, which it did.

When I was close to Dublin I came upon the River Liffey. The first thought that ran into my head was to wash myself in it before going into the city. I had my shaving gear with me. I went down to the bank of the river, found a spot that wasn't too deep and shaved myself in style. I don't think I had any mirror. I washed my feet, which was just as well because after the journey from Graigue my socks were so stiff with sweat that they could walk for you. I don't know if they were dirty but they certainly were sweaty as a result of all the miles I had travelled, two hundred and fifty altogether, on a bicycle that was no great shakes. And still I wasn't tired.

Having washed and cleaned and taken the weather-beaten look off myself I headed in for the big city. I had no problem making my way because I had the map. It reminded me of nothing but Tom Crean, the man from Annascaul who accompanied Scott to the South Pole long ago. I met Crean myself when he was a fairly young man. Upon my word I felt that the map which I had was every bit as important as any map they had when setting out for the Antarctic.

I cycled to Dublin again the following year, 1937, but my old pal Seán de Brún was with me on that occasion. We took the same road and stayed in practically the same houses. Having spent a couple of days in Dublin we struck south. Down in County Wicklow there was a house for priests where there was a great friend of mine, Bishop Ó hUallacháin, a native of Ballinrannig. Of course he wasn't a bishop then, just a young priest.

We spent a night there and honestly we spent more time talking than sleeping. The next day when we were ready for the road Fr Ó hUallacháin came out to the door with us. He put his hand in his pocket and handed me eight shillings. Full of cuteness and manners I pretended I didn't want to take the money! As the man who said it said: 'Take it away from me, though there is nothing I want more.' He did nothing but threw the money on the ground. There was no point in arguing, so I bent down, gathered the money and put it in my pocket. We said goodbye to him and headed across country through Kilkenny. We never stopped until we got as far as Clonmel.

It was then too late to go any further so we went looking for lodgings and found a place. We were shown the room, a small one that didn't look great. There were eight people sleeping in it, each with a single bed. The beds were in a circle around the room and in the middle wasn't there an empty bucket! However it didn't remain empty for very long with people getting out to it during the night according as they were short-taken.

Says Seán de Brún to me: 'If you have anything in your pocket put it under your head just in case because you don't know where you are.'

Three shillings was all I had left and he had two pounds. That was enough for us. Do you know how much we had to pay next morning? Sixpence each!

The next day, which was Sunday, we were in Cork in time for the All-Ireland Football Semi-Final between Kerry and Laois. We got the night's lodgings from friends of my own in the city and weren't charged a penny. Then there was our last journey, from Cork to Graigue. We made two halves of it and spent the night in a house west of Killarney. When we reached Graigue on Tuesday we had travelled five hundred miles and the amount of money we had spent wasn't worth talking about. It is a pity I am not as thrifty as that nowadays.

I remember well that journey from Cork, and with good reason. The Monday was fine and warm. Maybe it was too warm for some of us. Shortly after leaving County Cork behind us we saw a public house on the side of the road. Says Seán de Brún to me: 'I'm parched with the thirst. I'll have a bottle of lemonade.'

'Damn it I'll have another one myself,' I said.

In we went. The woman of the house was inside. Seán ordered what he wanted, and asked me: 'What will you have, Tomás?'

It was the devil and no one else who tempted me. Words came out of my mouth that had never come out of it before.

'Johnny,' said I, 'I'm going to try something that you never saw me drinking. My good woman,' said I in English, 'give me a pint of Guinness, please.'

What did my companion do but make the Sign of the Cross on himself! That was the first intoxicating drink I ever put into my mouth. I thought it tasted terrible. Still that terrible taste didn't last because after that I got a real liking for it. I didn't have a second one that day because I hadn't the price of it. I was just a little over twenty-five years then and fit to marry, but I see fellows nowadays and I don't know if they are even in petticoats when they have a pint on their head.

None of the local lads ever thought of anything else but football, football, football all the time. We would go anywhere to play or to watch a match. God be good to my mother, a bag of wind she used call the football and she could never understand why we were interested in kicking a bag of wind. I had the makings of a very good footballer myself and often wore the Ballyferriter Parish jersey, but I could never be any good because I was never given the right support, and by that I mean food. We hadn't the proper nourishment, and our stomachs were gaping wide because we had little to eat except potatoes and mackerel.

Whenever a football match was played in Ballyferriter with two or maybe four parishes against each other there was always wrangling. There were six parishes in all – Dunquin, Ballyferriter, Marhin, Keel, the Parish O' Moore and Ventry. English-speaking Ventry I call it, because any time the Ventry lads played in Ballyferriter English was the language which they spoke as they threw the ball around. But there were, and still are, people in that parish who have as much love for their own language as anybody else.

The Ballyferriter football field was very small and full of ragwort, but even so we never noticed it. As soon as ever the ball came in our direction it was just a case of catch and kick it. There was no sideline. There were no markings. Everything was a matter of guesswork and keeping the ball inside the fence and inside the spectators. The field was so narrow that the spectators were always in the middle of it, but the parish priest An tAthair de Brún, may his glory in heaven increase, was always there with his umbrella folded in his hand, as he shouted

'Keep back! Keep back!' His task was a hard one, however, because a fight often broke out among the spectators. You would see people with their fists raised high in the air hitting one another, not through pride, not through dislike, not through hate, but with heart and the hope that their own parish would win. The poor creatures who used to cause the ructions were harmless but they were full of spirit. As for prizes we didn't get even a cup of cold water out of the games, whether we won or not.

An awful change has come over Ballyferriter Parish since then. It is not the same place at all because football is a thing of the past there. It is the pub and not football that occupies their minds. They are nice and gentle and kind and honest, but where is the sense in going into a pub on a fine summer's evening instead of getting a football and going out playing? The one thing that stood to us was that we had no money.

10
ARMY VOLUNTEERS

At the end of the year 1938 I jumped on my bicycle one day
and went to Ballyferriter for want of something better to do. I
dropped into the post office. There was a group of young lads
there before me who were all set to go down to Cork City on a
recruiting course for the Volunteers. The Volunteers were part-
time soldiers that were set up in the year 1934 as a back-up for
the regular army. They used to do a short training course first
of all and after that they went back on a reserve training course
for a month every year.

The lads began coaxing me to go with them, and I promise
you it didn't take much coaxing to entice me. Of course all they
wanted was to have a bit of fun and I was always good for a
lark.

I thought of the sergeant in Macroom and of what he said
to me. Maybe the best thing I could do was to take his advice.
What did I do but leave the old bicycle to one side and ask a
friend of mine to bring it to Graigue sooner or later and tell
them at home where I had gone.

Of course none of the army authorities knew I was coming
because I hadn't been called up, so the lads pointed out to me
that I would have to go to Tralee Barracks first and tell them
there that I wished to be a Volunteer. Then we had to part. The
lads went straight to Cork with their papers. I was bound for
Tralee.

I went off just as I was. I didn't come home for this or that,
for clothes or boots or razor or soap. I had no money either, but
that was nothing new. I was as poor as the day I was sent to the
baptismal font, because I know that I had to get the loan of a
half-sovereign from somebody in Ballyferriter who himself has
gone the way of truth this long time. Praise be to God I paid
him back afterwards.

What happened in Tralee was that they accepted me into
the Volunteers for a month's recruiting course, but I am afraid

I was registered in English because the officer in charge of registration had no Irish.

There was no danger of losing my way in Cork because I had been there before that with An tAthair Tadhg. Anyhow I called into the barracks and the first person to meet me inside was a man whom I knew, Sergeant Tomás Ó Flatharta from the Aran Islands. A couple of years before that it so happened that Pádraig Ó Cochláin, a Corkman who was in charge of Clann na hÉireann, an organisation for young boys interested in Irish, gave me an invitation to go and spend a fortnight or three weeks with them in a summer camp in Ring in County Waterford. That was where I first met Ó Flatharta. He was on loan from the army to teach the boys gymnastics. He was a native speaker of Irish. I understood him well, he understood me and we got on fine. He used to take the odd drink. I myself had begun to drink at that time. That was the bad beginning.

Anyhow he gave me a thousand welcomes and instead of bringing me in and giving me something to eat he in fact brought me out! And instead of going back in again that night as I should have gone I had a dozen Guinness under my arm for the lads from Ballyferriter who had returned before me and were waiting patiently for the harum-scarum to come. The harum-scarum came and great God of Graces, if you only saw the welcome which I received when I said to them: 'Have a bottle, lads. You don't always have the likes of me around.'

Think of it, my first day ever in the Volunteers, I brought in an armful of bottles. How was it that I wasn't charged and thrown out? If I had been thrown out I wouldn't have encountered the hardship and the trouble that I had to endure for the following six years. Anyhow I was accepted.

The following day we all got up and were directed to the quartermaster's store. We were given a new rig-out, a uniform from the cap to the socks, a gun, and a bayonet, I am afraid. I suppose that the first time ever I cried bitterly and genuinely was when I was handed the bayonet and was told that it was for stabbing a person in the belly, and that I would have to learn how to do so. Bad and all as I am I never in my life dreamt that I would have to kill someone, but I am told that you would have to do it to defend yourself when there is a war on. Praise be to God I steered clear of the war and never saw anyone being stabbed. Nor did I do so myself either or even attempt it.

Three days I think we were in the Volunteers when we got our first pay. I will never forget it. Six shillings and two pence was all we got for the couple of days. Captain O'Connell was the one who paid us and I had the misfortune to put my two hands on the table while waiting for the few shillings and sign for them. He said to me in English: 'Take your two hands off the table and stand to attention!'

However when he really got to know me later on and found out that I was a native speaker of Irish we became as friendly as a cow with a cock of hay because he was very interested altogether in Irish.

That course lasted one month and I promise you that we didn't do much training because we hadn't any great liking for it. Some of us already hated the life. Nevertheless before the end of the month we were told that anyone who wished to come back after Christmas to do a three months' course, not in the Volunteers but in the army itself, would be welcome and would get a stripe. That was some honour, a red stripe across your arm or on your shoulder to tell you that you had the authority to hit a fellow who had no stripe!

The pennies were very scarce. Thirteen shillings and two pence a week was all we had, and if a volunteer was fond of anything, even a sweet cake or a smoke, not to mind the drink, the pay wouldn't last two days so we had to stretch it. Of course we weren't as wasteful then as we would be now if we had it.

By the time the month's training was over Christmas was at hand, and I came home to Graigue. We had a great Christmas wherever the money came from. I hadn't much time at home, however, because the day the three months' course started was 12 January. I returned but there were two or three others from the locality who did not, and in a way I don't blame them. I myself would have preferred not to go back. There was no obligation on me. Nobody was obliged to go back and anyone who did so went back of his own free will. That was the first course I did in the army itself, and honestly, talking about courses, I have done as many courses since then as Mick the Miller the famous greyhound did. But hardly anything came out of that really tough course because we never got the stripe that would give us the authority of a corporal and enable us to bring the tunic and the bit of red tape to the army tailor to sew it on our arms. That was not to be but we got something else out of the course. Anyone who wished to be an officer in the Volunteers could do an examination and if successful he would be called to the Curragh. That was a great honour.

It was the same old story again, back home to Graigue in April, going and coming and collecting food, as the old saying goes. There wasn't much to do around at home. I whiled away what was left of the spring. The summer came. There was the odd job to do but no real work, only pottering around. There was a bit of turf to cut, a small amount of hay to save when the time came, and then An tAthair Tadhg, God be merciful to him, and the boys from Farranferris. I used to be as happy as could be when I heard that they were coming because we always had great sport while they were amongst us.

11
THE CURRAGH OF KILDARE

Anyhow rumours of war were coming and we were preparing for it. I knew that I would be called up because the army had a hold over me. Sure enough I was called, and not only me but many more besides. We got orders to go to Cork again at the beginning of September. The world and his mother were in Collins Barracks but we spent little time there. I don't think we even got a bite to eat. We just went in, signed our names on a piece of white paper and headed for the special train that brought twelve hundred of us up to Loughbrown near the Curragh and over the fence from where the big horse-races are held. We set up camp there.

There was a great number of soldiers there, young and old. The most of them were young, about twenty years of age. We had little huts or bivouacs, row after row of them. We used to feel very cold at night and were always looking for extra blankets. But the hunger was worse than the cold. The rule in the army at that time was that you got your last meal at half past four in the afternoon and that was the end of it, and your stomach would be yawning until next morning. You may be sure if we had money we would have had food because it was easy to buy it. The Curragh was a couple of miles away; it was easy to walk there, and there was plenty of food on sale. I was surprised that I wasn't thrown into jail myself because in the evenings when it was dusk I used to go up and down between the two rows of huts, all the time shouting out like a fellow fit to be put into the asylum.

'Oh, the starvation!' I used to say out loud to see if anyone would come to help me but no one did.

Horse-races were often held at the Curragh, especially on Saturdays, and I hated the life so much that whenever I heard the noise and the clapping I used to stretch out on the bed instead of looking over the fence at the action. That is the way with the man of no means. The fact is that if we had the money we would have been enticed over the fence and would have met the bookmakers. But bad and all as the life which I have led has been I never fell in love with gambling, thanks be to God forever. Some of us hadn't even the clothes to wear going out. As far as drink was concerned we could afford to buy only the cheapest kind, the stuff which they used to call Johnny Jump Up or Lunatic Soup, and it can be truly said that many is the man it drove out of his mind.

Every day we used to leave the camps and go out into the countryside on manoeuvres, stealing up on each other from fence to fence and from bush to bush just like a hunter trying to raise a hare. We were for all the world like that crowd in America called the Bushbeaters because they believe that God is to be found in the bushes and they try to put him out by beating the bushes.

A farmer met us one day and said to us: 'Haven't ye killed the fox yet?'

That was pure sarcasm, of course, because the army had permission to go through anyone's field, even a field of oats or wheat, and he couldn't do a thing about it but allow us to go ahead because the law was on our side.

It wasn't long, however, until the call that some of us were expecting came, the call to do the officers' course which we had been promised when in Cork. We didn't go far away to do that course, only up to Pearse Barracks which was on our doorstep. Who should be with us but the Pearse Regiment, men who had jobs in all the universities around the country, even Queen's University in Belfast and Trinity College in Dublin. There was a big difference between some of us and those fellows. There they were with their big expensive cars, having come down from Belfast and over from Dublin, and every weekend – we were always free on Saturdays and Sundays – they would head off home, and God help the ordinary poor devils! They had to stay on, put their heads under them and stick their fingers in their mouths.

That course was different altogether to any other course. It was a queer set-up that you could become an officer in four months. The ordinary officer in the army had to spend two years in that same place. What made them think that I and others like me were so smart that we could squeeze two years' learning into four months?

When the course was over we hadn't made any headway at all as far as rank or standing or pay was concerned. It was the same story, thirteen shillings and two pence a week. I guarantee you we were fed up with the whole business because we had to get up very early every morning and the cold there was awful.

Every blade of grass is green until Christmas, as the old saying goes, but that I think is true only of Kerry because it was always cold in Kildare long before Christmas. That made little difference as far as animals and stock were concerned because they were indoors not outdoors, and they were fed indoors too, not like the creatures we had at home that we used to herd back on the hills where they couldn't escape the bad weather.

We were called out one morning in an emergency to beat all emergencies, as you might say. We jumped into the lorries, three or four of them and, oh Mary, it really was cold. We were wondering what was going on until we came to this particular place. We stopped and everyone jumped out. Then we saw this big fearsome thing with two or three men around it. We were ordered to stand in a circle. There was this monster, and the team who were going to give the demonstration were inside in the centre as we with our mouths open waited to see this wonder of wonders. We were told it was a tank and were informed that the reason we were there was to see how it worked. After a while a man got into it and then another man.

The noise started. As you might expect we made a gap for it to pass through. But I am afraid that the noise had only just begun when it stopped again. The tank had broken down. It was as dead as a doornail. As the old woman in Graigue said long ago, when talking about the cow that was weak from hunger and then died: 'She lay down, farted twice and died.'

That was the sort of tank corps which the Irish army had in 1940. I don't suppose that they got it going ever since, because I have heard, and I believe it, that it is still in a gap in some field up in Kildare, doing its job of keeping the hares out and the cows in.

Things were going all right until we hoisted our sails down to Waterford City. I cannot say what business we had there because we brought no freedom to Waterford, nothing but mischief and devilment. We used to eat the face off one another quarrelling any night that we had a bit of money but our numbers had been greatly reduced by this time. Many of the lads had left the army altogether and there were more officers than men left. It was still the same old story as regards training, going out into the countryside in the morning, searching, peeping around, stealing up on one another, firing shots as if to kill someone. But nobody was killed, praise be to God, from beginning to end. The training on the square was the same too except that a fellow could arrange his duty to suit himself until he had to do night-watch, and wasn't it strange that from the very beginning until the day I left the army I never had to do night-watch, however I managed to avoid it. I suppose they didn't trust me, because they were afraid from what they knew of me that if the enemy came, far from calling for help, I would invite him to come in.

12
OFFICER MATERIAL

In the middle of the following summer 1940 a great change
came over my life as far as the army was concerned. I and three
or four others got wind of the word that our days with the
Twelfth Battalion were over and we were to be transferred
very soon. So it was. We were sent to Collins Barracks in Cork
City. They were ready for us there and the big shot, Major-
General Costello, bestowed an honour on us on the night of
that same day. Having taken an oath to be faithful to the Con-
stitution and to Ireland we were made officers. From that day
on my feelings had changed. Whatever the other lads felt I
knew in my heart, and it wasn't because of my weakness, that
I wasn't meant to be an army officer.

Anyhow we were ordered to go into one of the biggest
shops in Cork, the Munster Arcade, to get a uniform. What I
got – it amounted to quite a lot – cost, I know, forty-five pounds.
You just couldn't imagine the commotion there with tailors
measuring us, backside and belly and head, tapes and chalks,
my dear man! Hundreds of pounds coming in from the white
cow's tail to pay for the rig-out – leggings and shiny boots, a
belt, and a cap that cost fifty shillings. The gloves which I got
were made of leather, but it was the belt across my body that
really made a big shot out of me. That belt was estimated to be
worth a thousand pounds because any woman who married
an army officer was considered to have got a dowry but people
don't think so nowadays. One overcoat wouldn't do at all so
we got two. And years before that, when I badly needed an
overcoat in the College north in Mayo, I hadn't even one, and
I was perished with the cold!

My life was different now. Instead of training I was doing
a kind of survey on those who were teaching the recruits as
they joined up, and I guarantee you there were people teaching who should really have been learning. The recruits were
joining in large numbers and an old woman would get a stripe

at that time.

Shortly after that I was transferred to Sarsfield Barracks in Limerick. I was annoyed that having been made an officer I couldn't come home to see my parents because no matter where I was I would always give my two eyes to come home. I begged the authorities to let me go for a day or two and in the end they agreed. I didn't come empty-handed. I had a gramophone, the first new one ever in Graigue, and a bottle of whiskey. That was my first homecoming as an officer, and I frightened the life out of them with the clothes I was wearing. Even my poor father didn't recognise me. Having looked at me twice he said: 'You're never my son!'

When he recovered he sat down. I planked the bottle of whiskey at the top of the table – I didn't hide it from him – and then my relative and neighbour, Cáit Bheag, whom I have already mentioned, walked in. She put her hand over her eyes when she saw the get-up of me sitting in the chair, white trousers and red leggings and brown boots all matching. I can tell you that there was no cow-dung on them. There couldn't be because it was a sin to dirty them. And then there was the belt across my belly and the mark of my rank on my shoulders. The poor woman was just as well off not to know what they meant. Then she spoke and the words came naturally from her: 'You're not Tomáisín!'

I pretended nothing for a while. She looked at my father then because herself and himself were always sparring with each other.

'Is that your son?' she asked.

'Won't you look at him again?' my father said.

'Aren't you quick with the tongue?' she said. 'You're just the same as you were the day you came into the world, when you caused ructions.'

'That day is gone,' my father replied. 'But won't you tell me who he is?'

She moved up close to me. The poor woman was sort of short-sighted. She stretched out her hand to me and I spoke. She recognised me then.

How clothes can change a person's appearance! It is fair to

say that the tailor was a good judge because when he sent you a bill demanding his money the words at the top of the bill read as follows: 'Clothes make the man.' The duds might make the same difference because if you wore them today after having worn a fine new suit yesterday maybe nobody would recognise you. Anyhow there I was that day, and famous and all as Lord Kitchener himself was he can hardly have been as proud of his uniform as I was.

Not long after that I got permission to come home again. Off I went by train. I got out in Dingle and who should be waiting for me but my sister Nell of all people. We hit the road home on our two bicycles.

I was a big shot. All you had to do was to look at me and my buckles and belts. Anyone would think I was about to be hanged. They were around my neck and around my belly and around my back. I was so gentle and well-behaved with regard to drink that I didn't go into any pub. I just looked left and looked right the same as I did in the army when I was told to.

It was dusk as we passed through Ballyferriter. You could just about recognise a person coming towards you if you knew him. A short distance west of Ballyferriter with Nell ahead of me we met a priest. My two eyes were always very sharp, many thanks be to God. As soon as I saw this priest something told me that I had met him before. Who was it, wending his way towards us, but the man who was president during my time in Wilton, the man who told me I wasn't to come back. I got off the bicycle and spoke.

'God and Mary to you, Father!' I said.

He stopped. Clearly I had startled him.

'Who have I?' he said.

'I'll tell you, Father, someone you had under your hand once upon a time: Tomás Ó Cinnéide.'

Before saying anything further he held out his hand.

'How are you, Tomás?' he said.

'Great altogether, Father,' I said answering him.

'Where are you going, or is that your wife?'

'I'm going home, Father, and that's not my wife. That's my sister.'

'You're in the army,' he said.

'I am,' said I, 'and I have the look of it.'

I called on Nell to come back, and she did. I introduced her to the priest and we were talking for a little while. I then told him that I would have to be going, which was true because I was very eager to see my parents. Said he to me before we parted: 'Tomás, would you feel like coming back to us again, because we'll accept you?'

'A thousand thanks, Father, but until the Day of Judgement I won't go back. Neither deer nor eagle will ever again see me in Wilton.'

After I returned to the barracks in Limerick again the joke of it all was that I was sent to Ardnacrusha to take charge there. I had in or about twenty men with me, and our means of defence consisted of seven or eight bags of sand with an old Lewis gun planked on top of them that wouldn't bring down even a heron if she came along. When I used to say that to certain people, however, they were anything but pleased.

On one occasion in Rineanna in County Clare we were digging down into the ground because we had got a warning that the Germans were coming. I said to the lads in my care: 'Ye're mine, and if the enemy comes I'll be with ye, and I'll tell ye what to bring with ye, the lightest things ye have, the little white shoes and nothing else. If the chase comes from the west we'll run east, but may God look down on us if it comes from the east because if we run west we'll be drowned.'

It was true for me because there was nothing to the west only the sea.

One night I was orderly officer. On my rounds to see if everything was all right I came upon my sentry, the person on whom everyone in the barracks depended. You would never believe the type of watch he was keeping. He was lying in a heap fast asleep on the sandbags, with his gun alongside him. He was snoring. There was a rule to deal with that kind of negligence if a country was at war, and the punishment meted out to a fellow in such a case was that he be shot in his sleep. But oh God, how would my conscience be today if that law was in force in Ireland at the time? Even if it was I don't think

76

I could carry it out. Our form of punishment was that the man be court-martialled and as a result of his court-martial he might get six months' imprisonment. Do you know the punishment which I handed out? I gave him a lash of a kick in the backside and if he didn't jump to his feet no little mouse ever yet got up to run away from the cat. I don't know what words he said because all I did was to run so that he wouldn't know who kicked him. I'm telling you he came to his senses good and fast.

Because I had got the belt of authority I had to be a little bit strict. There was no point in joking because my superiors weren't joking, although to tell the truth they didn't know a whole lot. Some of them were as ignorant as a crow's arse about education, about military matters and about everything else because they hadn't got the education. Many of the officers who were in the army in 1922, '23 and '24 were officers during my time and they hadn't got a day's schooling. There was one thing though. They were probably brave enough with a gun when they were fighting the English, and later on too, unfortunately, when they were fighting each other. Some of them left me in no doubt about their authority, and day after day I had to take orders from them. Not as much as one of those above me in rank had a word of Irish in his mouth, but, thanks to God, many of my own colleagues had Irish. There were three from this area in the same company as myself as well as another man from Tralee who was also fluent in the language.

I remember another night when I was orderly officer. Wherever I was I got an urgent call. Thank God I wasn't asleep because that could be thrown in my face afterwards. I was told that a soldier had come in who had a drop of drink taken and wasn't conducting himself too well. He had been absent without leave for a day or two. As soon as he saw me he came to his senses. He knew that he deserved to be punished, but I knew too that he was human and that maybe the same thing had often happened to myself.

I spoke nice and gently to him. He listened. By right I should have locked him up until he was tried next morning. All I did was to rouse the sergeant, who was in charge of beds and bedclothes, out of his bed. He wasn't at all eager to get up at the time. He thought that he himself was a big shot. He had a very sleek, very narrow, very thin moustache. I knew that he thought a lot of himself and that he had notions about his good looks. I couldn't care less. I had the authority to tell him to look after the man who was drunk so that he would get a night's sleep, which he did. I met the same soldier years later and he was so thankful to me that he would put drink down into my shoes if my shoes could hold it. The poor man couldn't be accused of anything because he was too innocent and I couldn't punish him because it wasn't in my nature to do so.

I got to know a good number of people while I was in Limerick, especially one particular family consisting of just the father and the mother, a son and a daughter. The son was young, about twelve years or so, but the daughter was grownup although I was a few years her senior. They invited me to the house. I went there and not just once either. The parents were so friendly towards me that they gave me the key to enable me to go in under the roof of the house any time I liked, whether they were there or not, whether they were asleep or awake.

The daughter had some connection or other with a tennis club and one day she invited me to go there with her, which I did. After a while she introduced me to some of the members. I was invited to play a game. I agreed although I had never before set foot on a tennis-court.

As for that stick that they have when playing – it would skim milk for you – there is nothing to it except to hit the ball when it comes to you, no matter where it hops.

Upon my word I was doing fine, so she thought. Then she put a question to me: 'Tell me, Tomás, where did you learn this game?'

'Well, Mary,' said I, 'I won't tell you a lie, and God forbid that I should. When I reached the age of twenty-one do you know the present my father gave me? He built a tennis-court for me in Graigue.'

I had to explain to her where Graigue was and what sort of a place it was, what kind of people lived there and the wealth that was there, though you can take it from me that as far as wealth was concerned you would get plenty of fleas for a shilling in Graigue at that time. In her innocence the poor creature believed me, but later on when I had become more friendly with her and was getting to know her better my greatest fear was that the devil might tempt her to come to Graigue to see the tennis-court.

As the old saying goes, we could be talking forever until the little tongue fell out of our mouth, and still we wouldn't have said all we wanted to. Shortly afterwards we were transferred from Limerick out to big Dromoland Castle in County Clare. An Englishman owned the castle and I suppose he was short of money because he rented half of it to the army, and we took up our station there. Talk about a fellow thinking he was somebody, himself and his knee-britches! He wouldn't even salute us in the morning he detested us so much. Why I don't know. He had five cars in the garage and he couldn't take even one of them out on the road because he was unable to get any petrol to run it. That used to break his heart altogether, not a drop for himself while the army had plenty of it.

The officers had their own rooms in the Castle but the soldiers were in timber huts. Of course I too had a room of my own, and whenever I was in that room I always thought of my father. If he heard or knew that I had a room in that big castle he would be very proud. Twenty years before that no Irishman of any kind would have been allowed in there, but that day had passed.

While we were in Dromoland the great manoeuvres began. The First Battalion from Galway City was to play the part of the enemy against us. They were described as the enemy because we had to pretend that we had the desire to kill. If you saw a soldier who wasn't on your side you were supposed to shoot him. Anyhow the battlefield was laid out in County Limerick and we were supposed to defend a particular place. The enemy came across the River Shannon from the north to face us, and whatever sort of a boat they had I am told that it had to make ten journeys to bring them all across. We could have drowned many of them if we knew it would take them so long.

When the two sides met we would remind you of Cú-chulainn or Oscar with our bravado. On clashing with the enemy our commanding officer's action was to start throwing stones at them and naturally I started imitating him. We were hauled over the coals about this later on but we got off because there was no criminal charge against us.

Anyhow I was captured together with the group under my command and we were put into an internment camp in a field. We had to stay there overnight but we were released the day after and went off home. We started out again the day after that. As the man said when he was flattened with a belt of a fist: 'Let me up and I'll have another go at the devil!' We were crossing a river. I am not too sure now what river but there was some kind of ford there. I took off my boots and put them under my arm. We crossed over, myself and a small group of soldiers with me, and I put aside the boots on the other bank. We were informed that the enemy was a couple of hundred yards down from us and that our task was to rout them. Some sort of skirmish ensued but when we came back down damn it hadn't Rommel's boots been stolen! That is all the enemy gained from their journey.

What was I to do then? Go barefoot to Dromoland Castle? Not at all. There was a house about fifty yards away and, what-ever possessed me to head for it and look for an old pair of boots, I knocked on the door. An old woman came out. The Lord have mercy on her soul, I know that she is dead by now because if she was still alive she would live forever.

'It is like this,' I said. 'My boots have been stolen and if you don't mind, would yourself or your husband have any kind of old boots that would bring me home?'

All she did was to start crying. I couldn't understand why until she recovered and told me that two days previously she had buried her husband. I sympathised with her respectfully and politely and prayed for his soul. She heard me and I sup-pose she thought that I was very sincere. She turned on her heel, went into a room and came back out to me with a fine pair of boots and a pair of socks. They fitted me so well that you would think they were made for me. They were black in colour but that made no difference as long as I did not have to go home barefoot. On top of that she made tea for me, while the lads were still outside waiting patiently on empty stomachs. That is the sort of officer I was, and yet there were people up in Dublin once a month writing a cheque for me as if they were blessed to have me.

Another day we were informed that we were to go on a long march and should bring everything we had with us, from the big gun to the small gun, whether they were crooked or straight, and I do know that some of them were as crooked as a ram's horn, that they wouldn't hit the enemy if he was only across the road from you.

Before we left the Castle we were told that we were going to Cork but when we got to the gate we turned right and never stopped once until we got as far as Lisdoonvarna on foot, and that is a long distance away. The springs frequented by people who suffer from rheumatics are close by. I saw them myself. I saw the people in them, but I wouldn't go into them even if I had rheumatics twenty-one times over. The smell from them alone would be enough for me. If the people of the town heard me I suppose that they would not be very thankful.

The next day we were ordered to get ready again. We set off south, on foot of course, in the direction of the place where we had started the day before, but instead of going back to Dromoland we in fact turned our backs on it. We were marching away ever and always for two and a half days until we reached Leamlara, a small place in east County Cork. More big manoeuvres were to be held there. I think that a group from Dublin were to be pitted against us and who of all people was supposed to come and inspect us the following day but the Taoiseach, De Valera himself, a hero whom I admired greatly ever since I was in petticoats.

We started digging holes – they were supposed to be trenches – in which to hide from the enemy. There was a soldier down in one of the holes with a pick-axe in his hand and bloody sweat pouring off him.

'Come up out of that!' I said to him.

He did so. I went down myself and struck a couple of

blows. I had never before done that kind of work. I jerked my back and fell in a heap where I was. I was hauled up, and a doctor and an ambulance were sent for to bring me to hospital in Cork. Just as I was going away who should I see coming down towards me with a group around him but De Valera, and it really broke my heart not to get the opportunity of shaking his hand or saying 'God be with you' to him. I was on the flat of my back, the big manoeuvres were under way and the shooting and the plundering continuing, but the hero had taken to his heels. That was thrown in my teeth later on.

I cannot say how long the fun lasted or who won, but one thing I will never forget is that two unfortunate fellows were drowned accidentally in the River Blackwater. One of them was a Kerryman and the other chap was from Tipperary. Didn't they pay dearly for their fun? The one consolation which their poor parents had was that the bodies were found and were buried in their ancestral graveyards.

When the rumpus in Leamlara was over a big parade was held in Cork and the two groups who were enemies before that took part. I got permission from the hospital authorities to come out to see the sight. That meant that I was on the side of the street watching them and clapping my hands when my own group passed by. I thought that there was no army in the world like them, just to look at them, a big long line of men, and when I saw the big guns and the small guns I thought there wasn't a doubt in the world but that they could beat Germany.

Talking of Germany reminds me that 'Lord Haw Haw' used to broadcast on the wireless at that time praising Germany and running down England. I am told that he was a Galwayman. Anyhow he mentioned us one night. I heard him myself with my own two ears, and I wasn't at all encouraged by him, especially since he was an Irishman. He said that the Irish army was so good that if they were all gathered together and sent to Puck Fair to rout the tinkers they would not be able to do so because the tinkers would beat them.

13
SOLDIER'S FAREWELL

I was attending to my business one day in Dromoland Castle when a soldier came in to inform me that the commander Colonel Henry wished to see me. He was a fine type of man if ever there was one. Upon my word my legs and hands began to shake when I heard that I was to go to see him. What did he want me for? What charge would he bring against me, since I was not aware that I had done anything out of the way. I dressed myself up smartly. You would need to do so when going to meet the likes of him. I went in. I saluted. He told me kindly to sit down. I did so. He did not call me Tomás but gave me my proper title.

'Lieutenant Kennedy,' he said to me, 'if what they say is true you're the one who knows all about cutting turf.'

My heart leaped when I heard the words. I was just ready to jump as a little bird in captivity would do when set free, because I then realised that there was no charge against me. I told him straightaway that I knew all that was to be known about turf as we had nothing else but turf at home but, believe it or not, I had never in my life taken a slane in my hand to cut a sod. Maybe I had taken a spade to cut top-sod on Minnaunmore, but as for slane-turf or bog-turf twelve sods high, we never had the like or if we had I didn't cut it.

The Colonel told me that the army had acquired a bog in Moanmore near Kilrush because coal was very scarce, and he needed someone like me to take charge of the work. We made the bargain and the next day I got a new car and a driver. Talk about importance! No wonder I was eager to be off. It isn't every day that Sallow Dan gets married or has the means to marry. I headed straight for Kilrush. My first task there was to get in touch with a solicitor, inspect the bog and arrange everything before the soldiers came to cut the turf under my direction, and God help us, they would be in a bad way if they were depending on me to handle a slane or clean a bog.

Having finished my business with the solicitor myself and the driver met a man on the street. The three of us started chatting. I told him that we would like to have a drink as we were thirsty.

'If a drink is what you want,' he said, 'go into Mrs Crotty's.'

If I live to be a hundred I will never forget that same house. Although I did not see the words written on the wall I noticed straightaway that there was nothing in the surroundings only welcome, friendliness and kindness. I later got to know the people of the house very well. I stood by them and they stood by me. Whenever I was free by day or by night I went there, not drinking perhaps because you did not have to drink anything to go there. Unfortunately they ran into bad luck after I left the army. Their son who was eighteen years old was drowned accidentally and from that day until the day the parents were buried the house wasn't the same.

Soon the whole battalion, about a hundred of us, was sent on the train west to Moanmore bog. I was in charge of the turf-cutting but there was a man higher in rank than myself in charge of the battalion. Still I was the big shot, as they thought, although I knew as much about cutting turf as I did about eating sand. There were people there from every part of the south of Ireland whose teeth were worn from cutting turf in their own native places and they could teach me how to do it, but you can't beat camouflage! There was I, the ganger who knew nothing about the work, moving up and down, smoking a cigarette while the boys burst their gut tossing turf up on top of the bank. We cut quite an amount there but things did not work out too good for us because the weather turned wet before the turf was dry and so it was sodden by the time it got to Dromoland. It served its purpose, however.

We spent another spell based in a small camp in Inagh, about twelve miles west of Ennis. Ennis wasn't a very Irish town. Yet there was a man there who was as Irish as Pearse himself. He was a teacher of Irish in the Vocational School. I got to know him and found him very nice and very friendly in every way. He invited me to the house, and of course I accepted not just once but twenty, forty and if I might say so, a hundred times. Every chance I got I went there and the family were so friendly with me that they told me to bring my best clothes along, those that I wore going to Mass or to a dance or any place like that, and they would keep them for me. I brought along everything I had except the duds which I used to wear around the place. I almost used to wear them in bed.

There were three daughters in the house, all very nice girls. One of them put her eye on me and I put my eye on her too. I spent a while flirting around with her. Everything was going fine. We understood one another and it looked as if we would have been happy to be buried in the same grave.

I had a bicycle and so had she, and we arranged to meet this particular night on the road halfway between Ennis and Inagh. I set out from the west hoping that she was setting out from the east. When I reached halfway I expected to meet her any moment. It was dark but that did not matter. We would recognise one another easily by day or by night. I was cycling along east at my ease but there was neither trace nor tidings of her. I found that very strange entirely. I knew that she hadn't let me down because she wouldn't do the like. I spent quite a while up and down the road outside Ennis trying to discover what had happened to her. In the end I lost patience and I went into the outskirts of the town where she lived. Who should I see only her father and brother looking for her all over the place. Obviously she was missing. They were looking for her because she belonged to them – she was their daughter – but I was looking for her because I fancied her and wanted to do a bit of flirting with her. Then I realised that she had in fact gone out to meet me, but where was she, or what mistake had we made that we missed each other? That was the question that even two could not answer. Of course fear would not let me ask her parents because my legs and hands were shaking. 'The reef is dangerous!' said I in my own mind, turning round and heading out west again for Inagh with my tail between my two legs.

When I reached the camp the first news which the sentry had for me was that a girl had been looking anxiously for me but that I could not be found. Having waited a long time for me she had to return home. But, Oh God of Graces, only later on I found out what happened when she arrived home. Didn't she admit that she had a date with me and that I didn't turn up! The next day the Ennis bus stopped just outside the camp gate. The driver asked some soldier or other if Lieutenant Kennedy was around. The lad told him that I was in the bog in charge of the turf-cutting but that I would be back home early in the evening.

'I have a few parcels here for him,' said the driver.

'Oh, they'll be all right,' said the lad. 'Leave them with me and I'll give them to him later on.'

He took the two parcels and threw them into my sleeping quarters. I came home in due course. When I saw the two bags my heart jumped for joy, something I needed after what had happened the night before. I was full sure I had got two presents until I took the twine off one of the parcels. The first thing I saw was a jacket of mine and a pair of boots underneath it, the best pair I possessed. It was then I realised my predicament.

'Your soul to the devil!' I said to myself, 'I've been thrown out and there's no hope of ever getting back in again.'

What had her mother done in a fit of temper? She had sent back every stitch of clothes I had in her house. That is what the Siege of Ennis did for me! I never since laid eyes on the house or on the girl and that was forty-six years ago. I would not fancy going to the house because the scalded cat fears the worst. A whistling woman or a cackling hen are two very bad signs, they say, and maybe the mother might whistle a tune for me if we met! As the woman said to me at home one day when I was fool-acting around with nothing to do: 'Haven't some people a fine life compared to others, whistling a tune on a scorching autumn day!' I was beaten again and there was nothing to do but return to the turf-cutting.

When we finished cutting we got notice that we were to be transferred to Ennis. We left Kilrush late in the evening, myself and about a hundred soldiers. The train was as slow as the Dingle train and that was slow enough for anything. It headed north first, naturally enough, following the railway line, and having gone a certain distance north it had to turn east towards Ennis. Would you believe it, it stopped in the middle of the bog about ten or twelve miles from Kilrush! We wondered what was wrong with it. Was there a cow or a donkey in its way that had blocked its path, or a bull that had gone astray? It was no such thing.

There wasn't as much as a squeak out of it because the light went out, the power failed, the life left it and it went on strike. It would not go any farther. We were told to get out and go looking for a stick like the one which you would put in a gap, or a fairly dry sod of turf or anything else that would make a fire to see if God would give it the heart to move. I think that we had been six hours there in the middle of the bog by the time it recovered. It farted once or twice, it took off and we blessed ourselves with joy.

It was well into the night before we got to Ennis, and maybe it was later still. In any case there were hundreds of people at the station waiting for us because the rumour had spread that the army was coming there for the first time. Most of them were young girls on the lookout for young lads because there is nothing to beat human nature. There were nice young lads in the flower of youth among us at that time. I remember well, as we marched from the station to where we were to stay, that the girls were coming along behind us in their hundreds and the song which the soldiers were singing was 'Goodbye, Dolly Gray!'

Many a thing is said that is not to be found in any prayer, as the old saying goes. This particular day it was my turn to be orderly officer. We were in Urlanmore not far from Rineanna at the time. Most of the soldiers had gone to Kilworth in East Cork where a competition was being held to see who was the best marksman in the army. Only a very few remained. The day was moving on when the officer in charge of the camp for the time being came to me and said: 'The cook is short two men.'

'Well,' I said, 'I can't help that because there's no man around I could order to go in and help the cook. Don't you know that every man who can walk is out training?'

'I know where there are two men,' he said, 'in the guard-room.'

'But do you know,' I said, 'why they are there? Those two have the itch and it isn't right to have them handling food.'

I felt that right was on my side. I had already heard that that disease was contagious.

'I'm telling you now, and this is an order from me to you, to send those two in to help the cook because he has nobody.'

'It's only a case of my word against your word,' I said, 'but I'll tell you the truth to your face. I'm not going to do it, and I won't.'

'I'll tell you again,' he said to me, 'and if you don't do it I'll show you that I have authority.'

'Do your best,' I said defiantly.

'Hand me your belt and your gun,' he said.

Maybe people might wonder why one officer would say those words to another officer, but what they mean is this. Any army officer if arrested or accused of anything was required to hand over his belt. That means that he would have no authority whatsoever left, because it seems that the power rested in the belt just as it rests in the priest's stole when he hears a sinner's confession.

I had to do as I was told so I threw him the belt with the gun attached to it. I was sent to my room and had no contact at all with anyone except the person who brought me a bite of food three times a day. I never left that room for a fortnight until I was summoned to a court-martial in Limerick. It is no exaggeration to say that on seeing all the officers involved in the case you would think you were in Áras an Uachtaráin on the day a new president was being inaugurated. They were as plentiful as the sand on the strand, and from all ranks. They were there from the colonel down to the lowest rank in the army, and there I was in the middle of them. It seemed to me that some of them were spitting at me.

The court sat and I was brought in like a little lamb. There was no need to put a spancel or fetter of any kind on me nor any rope around my neck either, because I was certain sure, and full of trust in God, that I would win the day against the fellow who had accused me. I gave the judge a true and accurate account of what had happened and why I refused to obey one of higher rank than myself. I let him know that it was not out of pity for the two soldiers that I wouldn't allow them in to handle the food but out of concern for the others who might eat it. However it was only on being asked by the court 'Why didn't you send for a doctor?' that I realised the mistake I had made. I know that if I had done so the doctor who was only a mile away in Dromoland would have backed me up.

I was brought to trial. They did not say whether Tomás was dirty or clean, innocent or guilty but I was set free for the first time in a fortnight. I spent another fortnight after that waiting anxiously for news. I wasn't locked up and had permission to come and go as I pleased. One evening a commandant who had no connection with the court beckoned to me. He was a nice friendly gentle man. The first thing he did was to shake my hand. That was the opening move. I knew that he was breaking the ice but that he had not as yet got to where the ice was thin. My heart jumped.

'Tell me,' I said, 'how much was I fined or was I fined anything?'

'Yerrah 'tis a thing of nothing,' he said. 'Five pounds.'

'Sure it is easy to make a collection,' I said, 'if everyone gave me a shilling because of their regard for me and because of the courage I had to do what I did.'

There was no more to it. It was left at that. Soon afterwards, however, a document with my name on it arrived. It was sealed tight and contained an order from a senior officer up in Dromoland that I would have to leave the army on a particular day. I then realised that I was about to be thrown out. The reins and saddle were to be taken from me, and when you see a horse running around a field without a reins or a saddle you may well say to yourself: 'There's a horse that is not in the race.' That was in May 1945.

I had spent almost seven years in the army. I admit now, and I have always admitted, that in a way the army was no place for me. It wasn't out of love of soldiering that I joined the first day. I joined for the want of a few shillings but with no

89

definite aim because I had nothing else to do only cavorting around Graigue. There was nobody at home to give me a shilling, not to mind a pound. Indeed no work was to be had even at the rate of a penny a day. I was unfortunate to have been made an officer by some sort of accident. Yet if I had enough sense I suppose I could have spent all my life in the army, but there was something telling me from the very beginning, even when I got the Sam Brown belt, that I would not spend my life there, because knowing the kind I was I realised in my heart and soul that there wasn't an earthly hope that I could remain on.

Army life is grand for a young person especially a fellow with a rank, but even the poor private at the present time is far better off, and not just as regards pay, than I was when an officer. The soldiers in my time had old tin plates as dinnerware and nothing else except a knife and fork and they had to remain outdoors until informed that the food was ready. That is not the situation nowadays. I am told that nowadays you go into a dining-room, you sit down and are waited on. Even the officers themselves scarcely got that treatment in my time.

I had great fun in the army because I made sure I would. There wasn't a rule that I didn't break and disobey but not so seriously that the whole country would know about it. There were fine people in the army and I found out who they were. Nothing annoyed me more than the rule that an officer could not go out and have a drink with a fellow who wasn't an officer. Praised be God forever I went out at night not only with the officers but also with the boys, the privates. They were fine decent lads and yet it was against the rules for me to be in their company. My own colleagues, the officers, often saw me in their company but they never reported me. They too often broke a rule themselves. Still and all I would never report them. My conscience told me that it wasn't right for me to break the rules but I am afraid I wasn't born a soldier and because of that I wore the soldier's uniform for only a short little spell.

I parted with the army and came home to Graigue as broke financially as I was when I joined. There was just one thing in my favour, however. There was an arrangement in the army whereby a small amount of money was put aside every month for officers, money which they could claim when leaving. A month or two after I had left the two hundred pounds due to me arrived by post. Believe it or not I put the money away the day I got it. I went out fishing that same night and we had fifteen hundred fish coming home.

14
ALL AT SEA

I had finished forever with the army but that was hardly any great loss to the country.

I was dawdling around Graigue with nothing to do during the day, and many is the time I didn't go to bed at all at night because I could afford to sleep until midday or later if I felt like it.

I was in Dingle one day during the November fishing season and heard about all the fish that was being caught in Bealbawn. Off I went on my bicycle and instead of coming home I went down the Cloonties road and across the strand to Bealbawn. I knew I would get a turn from someone. I had no fishing-gear on me any more than a child going out playing with his friends would have. The fishermen were just getting ready to put to sea when I came on the scene. They had a strange old custom that no crew would talk to another crew while preparing their nets and I did my level best to break it. There were about twenty fishermen on the pier and I was surprised by the frown they wore and the way they kept their heads down. When they spoke it was only a hugger-mugger among themselves. What did I do when I came along? I shouted out loud: 'How are the men of the sea?'

Not one of them saluted me. Whatever sort of a superstition was involved I don't know. Anyhow one of them came over to me and said: 'Would you like to go out fishing?'

'Indeed that's why I came,' said I. 'Of course I will.'

'But could you put on anything else except what you're wearing?'

'You don't mean to say that I'm naked,' I said. 'Haven't I clothes and boots on me?'

What had I but the white shoes I used to wear playing tennis in the army! To me they were just as good as wellingtons. I was put in the bow-seat and we started off as cocky as the best and the strongest crew there. Nobody at home had any idea where I was or what was keeping me, but that was nothing new. I had so many friends and neighbours and relatives in the locality – they are getting fewer now however – that I could call to any of them and stay the night with them. My poor mother was the one who worried most about me, yet she never became frightened or anxious whenever I failed to come back home. My father was out fishing and as for myself, instead of drinking or having a good time or squandering my money, I had got sense at long last. Then again maybe I hadn't. I was in the company of the heroes and people always thought a lot of anyone who was.

We didn't stay out fishing very long. Even so I had a string of mackerel coming home on the bicycle. Think of it, I had a bicycle to bring me home but the experts had to come home on foot!

That was the beginning of the November fishing season 1945 and, believe it or not, for a fellow who was never considered to be a fisherman I spent a whole season fishing that year.

We went out another night soon after that and there were scores of other currachs with us. They were there from Bealbawn. They were there from Ballydavid. They were there from Dooneen. We were searching away, casting out and hauling in, but there was nothing doing. After a long time we noticed that there was an odd currach heading for the landing-place and we realised why. There was nothing coming their way. Our own captain who was the oldest and the most experienced of us, said: 'We may as well go home, lads.'

Sound talk! I didn't object. The nets were hauled in and we went back to the landing-place. We hauled the currach up out of danger but we left her on her bottom because we had thought of another plan. We would go to Smerwick, drink a drop of tea and wait for the opportune time, that is the rising of the moon, or the *ré*. Some people refer to that in Irish as the rising of the *gealach*, the rising of the moonlight and there is nothing wrong with calling it that. Still I think that the correct term is the rising of the moon because the *gealach* is the light that comes from the moon. It is the moon that pops its head up.

It was always said that the fish rose with the rising or the setting of the moon.

The opportune time came. The nets were thrown on board and we rowed down to the mouth of the harbour. No sooner were the nets out than we could sense the fish getting caught in them. We let them at it and very shortly the captain said: 'We may as well haul in.'

They hauled in as fast as they could. I was in the bow-seat manning the two oars and did my utmost to carry out their instructions, when to row to the right or to the left. It was the will of God that we got the nets on board without any great delay. The currach was down to the gunwale.

Then we heard whistling and we then saw what the situation was with one of the other boats. It was too calm for them to be in danger of drowning, that is unless they were so stupid as to put too much fish in the little boat. Everyone knows that six good nets could bring in six thousand mackerel but the little boat could not take that much. One should avoid greed because many is the man who was led astray by it. Anyhow we couldn't go next or near that boat because there was no hope that we could put another hundred fish into our own little currach.

It was broad daylight as we approached Coosbuee. I never saw anything as frightening. The little currach was so low due to the load it was carrying that my head was level with the sea.

We rowed in. There were people waiting for us already because they knew that the boats which remained at sea had fish. We came in by the side of the slip on the water. We were counting the fish and taking them out of the nets at the same time, one man on the slip and two on board as we counted them.

A hundred fish was put into each bag and then handed up to me on the pier. As one of the bags was being handed to me I somehow fumbled it and it slipped from my grasp and fell into the water with a hundred big fat fish inside. The water was still twelve feet deep and nobody there was at all inclined to go under water to recover the bag. We had to wait until evening, when the tide had ebbed and the rest of the fish taken to Dingle, to recover the bag. We had no alternative but to divide it in three and salt it, and wasn't that the fine feeding! We had twenty-five hundred fish that night. We sold it in Dingle for little or nothing, only three shillings a hundred, and that was a terrible shame. I myself hadn't much more than a pound as a result of the night, but if you had a pound in those days you got value for it, and another thing, you wouldn't spend it as foolishly as you would a pound in today's money.

Another fishing season came then, the May season. Something I could never understand was why the men from this side of the parish always fished out of Coosnanay near Clogher instead of going to Bealbawn where the sea was calm. On a bad night there is scarcely a wilder or a nastier spot on the coast of Ireland than Coosnanay. It is a frightening place to land by day or by night if there is any swell at all there, in other words when it is not dead calm. There are two submerged rocks, the Northern Hag and the Southern Hag, and you would need to know where they are, especially when covered by water. It is a dangerous spot and the fellow who hasn't some little knowledge of it will end up there.

Another night myself and two lads from Clogher decided to go out. It was a fine night, a really fine one. The sea was like glass and there wasn't a ripple on the shore. We put the nets on board, started rowing and never stopped until we got as far as the 'light'. That is the place from which we could see the Tearaght Lighthouse. We put out the nets. The man with the pipe reddened it and had a smoke. The man who liked his cigarette pulled out one and lit up. There we were talking away. The nets were in the water which was grand and calm. Suddenly a thick fog came down. Darkness had scarcely fallen as yet.

The oldest man, the experienced one, spoke. 'We'd better haul in,' he said.

I was in the bow-seat of course because I knew nothing about any other place in a boat. They hauled in the six seine-nets.

'What will we do?' I said.

'Yerrah, the night is fine,' said the old fellow. 'Have a stretch for yourselves.'

'But,' said I, 'if we do where will we be found in the morning? Whatever about ye I'm going to stay on my two oars and keep on the move.'

'But where will you sail?' he said. 'Where's your compass?'

'I'll head for the Aran Islands,' I said jokingly.

You couldn't tell where east, west, south, or north was, the fog was so thick, but whatever put it into my head I felt I was going towards dry land. If only I could get a glimpse of some headland I would have an idea as to where I was.

The next thing I noticed was that the two others were asleep and one of them snoring just as if he was in the middle of his bed. I was foolish enough and stupid enough to keep on rowing and rowing, and where was I going? That was the question. I didn't care as long as I didn't fall asleep. Maybe I was too cautious and they were too careless. In any case I spent, I suppose, four hours rowing on my own, giving it all I had. At long last the fog lifted slightly and we caught sight of land. The other two were awake by this time.

'Many thanks to God,' said I. 'Maybe I'll get some relief now.'

'What relief?' said the man nearest to me.

'There are strips of skin gone off my backside,' I said, 'that are six inches long, and if you don't believe me put your hand there.'

We had reached land sure enough but where?

'We're very near Valentia Island,' says your man again jokingly.

'It doesn't matter a damn,' I said. 'We'll put ashore wherever we are.'

It wasn't long until the fog lifted altogether and then we found that we were still in sight of the Tearaght Lighthouse. We had to row from there to Coosanay and that is quite a distance. It was broad daylight as we came in and we were just as empty-handed as we were when setting out.

I love the sea. It is a mystery in itself, if only because of the coming and going of the tide, one of the things that Aristotle could not understand. It has a beauty and a charm about it and I think that there is no better way on earth of passing the time than to spend a fine day at sea. I was about six years old when first I went out and somehow or other I was never seasick. I am not saying that I am a fisherman. I wasn't any great shakes because even though I spent a lot of my time on the sea I was only clowning, not fishing. I suppose there is hardly any place in the world nicer than our own little harbour Coosnanay from which to put to sea, row back as far as Clogherhead and see the islands out west from you, the dead calm sea and not a stir nor a ripple on the shore so that you could safely let your currach drift and even if it struck a rock it would not be damaged. That would do anyone good.

We derive little pleasure from the sea on the day of a storm but the visitor who never before saw it enjoys it. The sea mostly comes from the north-west during stormy weather, wave after wave as high as a mountain, and to see those waves coming towards you, especially if it was your first time here, you would say to yourself that you had better make a run for it because they would drown the world. Nevertheless when they hit the shore that is the end of them. Every wave has to recede. That is a mystery in itself and when I look at it I find it strange that anyone could say that there is no God.

Of course the sea is treacherous and it took from us some fine people. It wouldn't show any pity or compassion for the Pope of Rome himself, important and all as he is, if his boat was capsized. He would be drowned just as fast as I would. As I often say:

> There is weakness of body and weakness of mind.
> Another weakness is to be too daring at sea.
> The sea is wild and often angry
> And it doesn't care who makes his bed in it.

It was and still is vital for anyone, whether a sailor or not, to be able to swim if going out in a small boat, especially a boat as frail as the little currach. Even though the danger was always there and the fishermen knew it yet they never made any attempt whatsoever to learn how to swim. There were two brothers living near the River Feoghanach in the Parish O' Moore, and they were excellent swimmers. They were day and night in the river especially in summertime, but of the thirty men who used to fish in Coosnanay not one of them could swim a stroke. They never went to the strand in their youth and it never dawned on them at all that it was necessary to be able to swim. The poor creatures who were drowned – I knew many of them, and maybe the sea wasn't the cause of their drowning but rather too much fish or an accident of some sort – if they were able to swim like other people they would have come home safely because they weren't too far out at all from land.

A man put a question to my father one day.

'Tomás,' he said, 'since you live so near the strand how often do you go swimming?'

My father turned his cap back. That was a sure sign that he was ready to chaw the rag. It wasn't due to any gale of wind blowing in his face.

'To tell you the truth,' he said, 'I hadn't a swim since the day I was brought to the baptismal font.'

Even we ourselves when young were not in the habit of going to the strand because there was no hope that our parents would go with us to teach us how to swim. Still and all I myself was able to swim in a sort of way.

I went into the water in Clogher Strand one day. All I had for a swimming togs was a piece of newspaper held with a twine around my body. I swam east and I swam west. I went north and I went south until a wave came that swept the feet from under me. My head went down and my legs went up. I surfaced again with my belly full of salt-water. It was then I noticed that the paper was missing. It had peeled off in the water but I didn't mind. I headed for the strand and who should be there before me but my neighbour and friend Cáit Leighin from Clogher with her mouth open back to her ears laughing at me. I was safe but the crabs could have had me long ago only that the God of Glory brought me in safely.

Some of the old people had no love of any kind of water. Quite often they didn't even wash themselves, and some of them had the signs of it on their faces, on their ears and behind their ears, because there was nothing there but wax, and it wasn't beeswax but dirt-wax. There were others, however, who were very particular about their skin and their bodies because they used to get a basin of water first thing every morning and a piece of soap and a cloth, maybe – very often they hadn't a towel – and give themselves a right good wash.

There were two brothers and a sister living in the locality and they had the name of being spotlessly clean. I used to call in to see them and was surprised to see that they always washed their hands before sitting down to table. But I am afraid that not everyone was like that because I know of people whose method of cleaning the plate after having a bite to eat was to wipe it on their backside. But that day is gone and every home nowadays had conveniences and appliances as good as you would get in the Skellig Hotel in Dingle.

The sea always reminds me of driftwood. Rack we called it. Since I was a youngster, and that is many a day and night ago, it was in my blood to have a craving for rack. The amount of rack that comes in here, though, is very small because the wind is usually from the west and when the rack reaches the islands it has to disperse either north or south. That means that not much comes our way. But the people of the Western Island often did well out of rack. They would go west to collect it whenever they thought it likely to come. They once made a fortune out of a ship that hit a reef near the Island. They even got watches from it, not to mind blubber and timber.

Rack often causes great jealousy, just as much as fish does. Whenever you got a piece of rack, be it big or small, you put it up safely out of danger from the tide and threw a stone down on top of it. That was your mark. The next person to come along and see the stone placed on it wouldn't touch it, that is unless he was a thief and so would put it under his arm or on his shoulder and take it home.

An innocent poor man went to confession once to a certain priest in Ballyferriter and he started off his confession by mentioning rack, that he went to the strand one day and saw a piece of rack with a mark on it. Greed got the better of him so he just slung the piece of timber up on his shoulder, brought it home and hid it. But in his innocence the poor fellow, having told the priest about the rack, went on to mention a girl whom he met one night and engaged in conversation.

I cannot say what thoughts entered his head, but in any case he put his two hands around her. She took fright and ran away from him – again I cannot say why – though she knew him very well. The priest, however, did not condemn him, but before giving him absolution he remarked wittingly: 'I suppose you thought she was rack too!'

One day I took the notion to go out looking for rack. I brought a bag with me. There was a light breeze blowing straight from the west and it struck me that there might be some rack to be got around Ballyoughteragh West. I went down the cliff to the west of the village and I guarantee you there was nothing there only bits of sticks. However I nearly filled the bag and when I had gathered all that was there I slung it up on my back. As I was coming east through the village I decided to call in to see a great friend of mine, a woman who had the same welcome for a tramp as for a bishop. She made tea for me. That of course was the very reason why I called in. I was fond of tea. It was scarce in some places and Graigue was one of them. Naturally out of good manners I left the bag outside the door.

'Where were you, Tomás?' the woman of the house said to me.

'Yerra, I was looking for bits of rack,' I said, 'and the few I got are in the bag outside.'

The young man of the house was present. After a while, as I was drinking my drop of tea at the top of the table, he went off out. I took it that he was going about his business. After eating and having a bit of a chat I thanked the woman of the house. It was the least I might do. I went out and slung the bag upon my back. It is a good walk from Ballyoughteragh West to the top of Graigue. I took the short-cut west through the Fair Ground. When I reached home my father was sitting in the corner.

'Where were you?' he said.

"I'll tell you,' I said, 'I was looking for rack.'

'Did you get any?'

'I did,' said I, turning the bag upside down.

The first thing that came out, before any splinter or any

stick, was two big stones that my rogue of a man in Ballyoughteragh West had put into the bag! Wasn't I the right fool not to realise the trick he had played on me? Since then I often meet that same man and every time he sees me he can't help sniggering, and the first question he asks me, pulling my leg, is: 'Tell me, Tomás, did you find out at all who put the stones into the bag? I've been trying to find out ever since who did it but I haven't succeeded as yet and I don't suppose I will now.'

And what answer do I make him?

'You black rogue, I hope that someone puts a load on you, not in the next world, God forbid, but in this one so that I can get my own back for what you did to me the day you made an ass of me with my load of stones.'

I was at home in Graigue one day long after I left the army, and who should ramble in but Artie Gloster. I first met Arty in the army, and he had the same desire to be a soldier as I had, and I assure you that was damned little. He could speak Irish and that is the main reason I took to him.

Anyhow when he was on holidays on the Island he dropped in to see me. It was a Sunday. We went to Ballyferriter and after having a drink we decided that I would go to the Island with him. We reached Dunquin Pier, went down to the edge of the water and looked around. There was no one going to the Island. We found out where a certain currach was, however, and a grand little currach it was too.

The man who owned it has gone the way of truth now, God be good to him, and that man was Kruger above anyone else in the world.

'Your soul to the devil,' I said, 'this is the boyo's currach. He's in Dublin himself, and we'll be back tomorrow or the following day before he comes home.'

We put the currach on the water and set out. I was on the bow-seat and Artie at the stern. He knew as little about the sea as a hen does about swimming, but at least I had him with me for company. He had one oar up in the air and the other one down to the hole for the thole-pin and that is no way to row, but the sea was calm. Halfway across he told me to stop rowing for all the world as if he was in pain.

'What's wrong with you?' I said.

'Hold on,' he said, 'we'll cheer ourselves up.'

He pulled out a long-necked bottle and it wasn't a bottle of water! Upon my soul I didn't object. I was the first to take a swig out of it, and went down a good distance in it. Then I handed it to himself.

'Do whatever you like with it now,' I said, 'but for God's sake don't stir in the currach. Stay where you are and I'll bring it in on my own.'

I knew where the tide was running and made for it because the tide is a great help. We reached the Island. There were roughly forty people living there at the time. When we landed we didn't have to put as much as a hand on the currach because the welcome we got, you could say, would carry ourselves and the currach up to the top of the Island. We were given a bite to eat and honestly whatever amount was left in the bottom of the bottle didn't last long.

Next morning the sea was dead calm but there wasn't a man to be found in the Island even if you paid him a hundred pounds. They were all out lobster-fishing, and there was I thinking of going back to Filemore while Artie was staying on in the Island.

Myself and Artie and six island women brought down the currach and put it on the water. I boarded it. I made the sign of the cross on myself like every fisherman that ever put out to sea, and got to Dunquin on my own, thank God.

I was just like Eoghainín Brún from the Island long ago. Eoghainín and two others were going back there one night. The other two had just got out of the currach at the pier when a wave came and swept it away with Eoghainín still on board. The wind was from the north so not surprisingly he went south but he had the sense to remain on board. Next day he and the currach were found near Valentia Island. It took him three or four days to come back to Dunquin on foot. By the time he turned up he had been keened over and over again, and do you think they welcomed him? Not at all. They were running away from him because they thought he had come back from the dead.

Anyhow when I got to Filemore there wasn't a sinner to be seen. The tide was out but was beginning to come in. I had to go looking for help and my main worry was that the currach might be afloat when I got back. Up the cliff I went like a hare with a hound after it. It was the luck of God that there were two men in the field across the road working at the oats.

'Hurry up in the name of God,' I said, 'before 'tis taken by the tide.'

'What will be taken?' says Micí Bán Ó Sé, one of the two, who has been living in Carhoo this long time.

'Kruger's currach,' I said, 'would you believe? I've just come from the Island on my own, but thanks be to God there's not a thing wrong with it. We'll do the talking below at the pier, but hurry up because the tide is coming in.'

We headed off down and it wasn't long until it was hauled up out of danger and tied up for a full year and a day, as they used to do with the boats long ago. The next time Kruger met me – he was a near relative of mine – I was about to thank him but didn't get the chance because he gave me pigs' and dogs' abuse. He ate the ears off me. I guarantee you I never since stole a currach.

15
LEARNING AND TEACHING

I was at a loose end as much as ever and hadn't a penny in my rag except for a day's work here and a day's work there. Then a little bird came with the news that a training course for teachers of Irish was due to start in Dublin in the middle of the summer. I sent off an application and received a reply stating that I had been accepted. I grabbed the chance with both hands and went off to Dublin. I got to know the other people on the course, two girls and eleven men. There was a girl from Donegal, a native speaker, but as for her Irish – and I am not criticising her – even the grey geese couldn't understand her.

The course started. It included English and Irish, some sort of mathematics, history and geography. It also included gymnastics but I couldn't see what purpose that served because I know that some members of the class couldn't put one foot past or across the other. There was a thing there called a 'horse'. That was a gadget used in gymnastics to prove to young people who could jump over it by placing their hand on the centre that they had no cramps. I myself had no cramps at the time. I know one man who jumped and got caught in the middle of the horse and as well as that didn't the little white pants fall off him! You would imagine that that would teach him sense as regards gymnastics but it didn't.

I spent some time searching for lodgings near the place where the course was being held. In the end I was told to try such and such a house, No 5, I won't say what street. I knocked on the door about three or four o'clock in the afternoon. The landlady came out and we were talking in the doorway. I saw a man inside reading a paper but couldn't see his face. I suppose he recognised my voice because no sooner had I gone into the room – he was still reading – than he threw away the paper and started laughing. Who was it but my friend and neighbour Micheál Ó Scannláin from Dunquin, who was teaching near the city and was staying in that house.

Anyhow the landlady agreed to take me and said that the charge was two pounds a week. And what was my pay during the course? Two pounds ten shillings a week! Isn't it a miracle, after the sort of life I had led in the army not to mind anywhere else, that I would have to live on a half-sovereign a week? In those days you would give a half-sovereign to a child on the day he was baptised

One thing that annoyed me was that the house was full of lodgers and we almost had to take it in turns to eat a bite. To get to the toilet, which is something everybody needs, we had to go back through the kitchen and that did not appeal to me because I was always very shy about matters of that kind and never liked anyone to see me going on such a trip. Even to this day no one sees me going there.

It wasn't long until myself and Micheál made up our minds to leave. There was an evening paper in Dublin at that time called the *Evening Mail* and every evening it used to carry hundreds and hundreds of advertisements. The upshot of it all was that we found another place. To tell the truth we tried not just one place, but two, three, four places, as we were quite particular, why I do not know, because honestly anyone who had spent a term in the army wasn't very demanding or particular about accommodation. If in the army you were told to lie down in the middle of a field you had to do it and spend the night there, something I often did.

There were three or four lodgers with us in this new house. The man of the house was a sergeant in the guards and the woman of the house was always at home taking care of the house and the meals. From the time she got out of bed in the morning until she lay down at night, whatever time that was, she had a cigarette in her mouth and never once put a hand to it. No wonder that half the cigarette consisted of ash as she handled the food. Then, supposing she was making a stew, the ash would fall down into the stew, and what did she do? She mixed it in. We never noticed the taste, however, because we were young and there was no limit to our appetites. In the Dublin of those days the fare provided by landladies did little to raise one's spirits. Still to give our landlady her due she was

105

a decent woman.

In the spring of the year 1947 there came a very cold spell. I suppose the like of it was never seen in Ireland before or since. It affected me more than anyone else and believe me I wasn't all that used to heat in Graigue although we always had a fine blazing fire of top-sod turf. When going to bed you didn't put on pyjamas although we had such things. You left on the trousers you were wearing, you put another one on outside it, and if you had the third one you didn't object to it. Still it was all to no avail because the cold got through. We were frozen. We were perished. When we woke up in the morning we were like fish that had been on ice since the night before.

The turf wasn't scarce at that time but it was drenched wet. It was so wet that even paraffin wouldn't light it. We used to have a sort of a fire early on in the night but about ten o'clock, if we were in, the fire would begin to die out and there was nothing left to put on it. I got an inkling that there was a shed at the back of the house which contained nice turf so I stole out the front door one night and went around to the back. I opened the shed door very quietly just like a fox would do. Nobody heard me, I thought, but just as I was counting the sods and gathering them in my arms someone let out a roar at me: 'What are you doing there?'

Who was it but the man of the house! If anyone was ever ungrateful to his legs I was. I nearly fell in a weakness. He couldn't say I was a thief because in fact I was dying with the cold, and in any case only a stepmother would blame me for bringing a few sods into Micheál who was waiting eagerly for a bit of heat. I went back into the room.

'Where's the turf?' says Micheál.

'Ask a certain part of me,' I said, 'but don't ask me politely. Don't you see the colour of me? Wasn't I caught with a bundle of turf just under my coat! I'll be damned lucky if I'm not up in court in the morning.'

There was nothing to do then but go upstairs, throw off the trousers I was wearing, put on the pyjamas I had in the army – I still had them – and put the second trousers on outside them.

I was reminded of the first pyjamas that had come to Graigue many years before that. I imagine they came from America. The people of this townland in those days knew little or nothing about such things. I am certain that some of them thought that they were a sort of trousers one wore on the strand when going for a swim or after a swim. They were never used until St Stephen's Day when the chap to whom they had been sent donned them and there wasn't a bit of him to be seen underneath. Someone asked him: 'Are you going to bed?'

He said nothing as neither he nor I knew what the pyjamas were for, but in any case he had a great day hunting the wren because he made a bit of money.

The day came when myself and Micheál left that house. We were going from house to house until we finally got a place on the North Circular Road. There was no landlady involved this time. We were fending for ourselves. We had our own room, our own furniture, our own cooking equipment, our own food. I was afraid of my life that with my income I would be unable to keep up with my companion who had a teacher's salary. A tramp would collect a hell of a lot more money in one day than I was getting a week.

We were as friendly as a cow with a cock of hay, and that is friendly enough for anything, but after some time we had a slight falling-out. One day passed, two days passed, three days passed. Sunday came and still we weren't talking. We went to God's Mass separately. We came home. I cannot recall now which of us had the heart to buy a rabbit for the dinner.

Micheál was the cook. He was better than I was. An hour or two before the cooking started the devil tempted me and I went off out. Anyhow wherever I went for a walk I came home about two o'clock with my stomach hitting off my backbone from the hunger.

'Well now,' I said to myself going up the stairs, 'even if he's not at home there is a bit of the rabbit left for me.'

I opened the door. There wasn't a sinner under the roof of the house. I looked over towards the fire, if you could call the contraption a fire. I saw some sort of a skillet with the lid on it.

My heart gave a jump when I saw the two ears of a rabbit jutting out under the lid.

'Ah yes,' I said to myself. 'There is half of it left at any rate.'

I lifted the lid, and oh God! How was it that I didn't collapse and stay there on the spot without a priest or a doctor? The head of the rabbit was there sure enough, complete with the two ears, but there wasn't as much meat on the head as would feed a sparrow. The body itself was missing.

'A big joke,' I said when Micheál came home.

He started laughing. Then we spoke. The row was over.

Day followed day but year didn't follow year because the year wasn't up yet. The teaching course ended, and I learned that the only qualification I had got was a qualification to teach Irish, and Irish only, because I had failed in English. As far as I know nobody else failed in English but I wasn't disappointed. If I had Churchill's English, and his English was famous, I do not think I would ever have spent my life teaching.

However I got the opportunity to earn a few shillings. There was a job as a school-cleaner vacant in Coláiste Mhuire, Parnell Square. Anything would be better than nothing. I called into the school and met a brother. I told him my story, how I had done the course, my spell in the army and this and that.

'I won't put you cleaning the floor at all,' he said. 'I'll put you teaching the boys instead.'

So it was. I had two classes every morning and taught them Irish and Catechism. As far as Catechism was concerned I was really the one who should have been learning it because whatever I had learned in school in Ballyferriter I had forgotten by then. Two pounds a week was my pay from the brother, and it wasn't much because no landlady would take you in at that time for under two pounds a week, and how much would I have left then?

I saw on the paper that a domestic economy college for girls in Cathal Brugha Street was looking for a temporary teacher of Irish, so I applied and got the job, a couple of classes every afternoon teaching Irish to young people who were learning how to cook and who had also to get a qualification in Irish. I guarantee you none of them had as much Irish as I had French. Nine shillings an hour I was paid and that was good money. If you only got two hours a day that was eighteen shillings, and there was no one alive at that time who could eat that much. Perhaps you might drink it if you were reckless enough and I often did, I am afraid.

One day towards the end of the class I was standing in front of the students as independent as could be. I had about five or ten minutes to go and I was talking away. Then the devil tempted me and I put my hand into my pocket. I pulled out a cigarette. I lit up. I put it into my mouth. As bad luck would have it who walked in but the inspector! He called me over to one side.

'Are you allowed to have a cigarette in your mouth in front of a class?' he said.

'I never heard I wasn't, sir,' said I.

'All right, ' he said. 'It is for me to make a decision. Go home now and stay at home.'

That finished me with Cathal Brugha Street. I had no further business in Dublin so I came home to Graigue and believe you me my parents looked anything but pleased when they saw me coming again, and I couldn't blame them. Many was the bite of food I had eaten there and hadn't paid for yet, although I intended that if I ever got on in life I would put them up on the top of the mountain. I felt miserable. I hadn't harmed or hurt anyone. Yet the horrible truth was that having grown up and spent half my life away from home I was back home once more and still dependent on my mother and father.

16
THE FARTING CAR

I wasn't very long at home when something possessed me to go off to Dublin again. I had great friends out in Clontarf. There was a son of theirs in the army with me, and when he introduced me to his mother and father they told me to come and stay with them any time I was in Dublin. I went out to the house and told them my predicament. In a way it was like a confession although I didn't tell them my sins. Wherever they got the information they were able to tell me that Bord na Móna were looking for men.

Next day I made straight for the Bord's office in the city. I was taken on and was informed that I would have to go to Newbridge this particular day, which I did willingly. I said goodbye to my friends in Clontarf, turned my back on Dublin and arrived in Newbridge. An employee of the Bord there told me that I would have to wait until the other five who were called with me arrived.

When the six of us assembled he told us the type of work which we were expected to do. However we would first have to do a short training course. Ireland was to be divided into six areas and each of us would have his own area. I had my ears cocked listening but I didn't have the hearing of a thieving pig. I couldn't care less where the others were sent. If they were sent to Timbuktu that was their business. This man was doling out the areas and when he came as far as myself he told me that I would have the title of Recruiting Officer, with an office in Killarney of all places! Oh God of Bright Graces, when I think of it now, I got all excited on hearing him mention Killarney. I could almost jump Mount Brandon.

'There's just another matter,' he said. 'You will need a car but you won't get one from Bord na Móna. You will have to buy or get one off your own bat, somewhere or other.'

That put me thinking, and I suddenly remembered the two hundred pounds I had got from the army. I still had it in safe keeping. With that money a friend of mine in Cork bought a car for me and I got a day or two off to go down from Kildare for it. In spite of all the years I had spent in this world there wasn't a hope that I could drive it. Anyhow off I went down to Cork and my friend brought me around his yard in the car once or twice. Then I told him that I had a good idea as to how it worked and the next day, after another short lesson from him, I felt I was doing fine and told him that I was quite capable of driving back to Kildare.

'I don't like letting you off through Cork on your own,' he said, 'because you might do harm to yourself or to somebody else.'

He sat in with me and brought me through the city and two miles outside it on the road to Kildare. We parted company there and I was very thankful to him. I set off with my two eyes taking everything in. I wasn't going too fast because I didn't know the road and wasn't used to the car. A short distance outside Cork a little cat took it into its head to cross the road as I was approaching. I heard the screech, I felt the bump and I know that that was the little cat's last day alive. It wasn't his fault but mine because I was green and knew nothing about cars.

I had no notion of stopping until I got to Newbridge. I cannot say what speed I was doing, but I do know that shortly after dusk I was still about ten miles out from my destination. I stopped and wondered if the car had any lights or if it had where was the switch.

I started searching. I could find nothing. I could neither press the switch nor pull it out. I couldn't push it east or push it west because I didn't know where it was. After darkness had fully fallen I had to travel about three miles an hour and it was the will of God that nothing came towards me that I might harm. At long last I reached the gate of the Bord na Móna headquarters. I stopped. There was a man on the gate.

'For God's sake,' I said, 'let someone else bring this car in through the big gate because I can't.'

The car was in great condition and people were jealous of me because they thought that I was really set up now that I was going to Killarney any day soon with a car of my own, that I was my own boss, and had a job for life. But I am afraid that things don't always turn out as expected. What happened was that there was a change of government very soon after that and we learned that some of the Bord's work was to be cancelled and so instead of going to Killarney I was sent to Connemara together with a man from Galway.

I remember well the day myself and the Galwayman left Kildare on our way west. I was driving along and chatting with him, as you would expect, until we came to this particular part of the road a good distance west. It wasn't a corner or a cross-roads, just a bend in the fence, and of course that meant a bend in the road as well. Maybe I was a little too far out. The next thing was that a big timber lorry came towards us which would terrify you even to look at it. It didn't pass me without saluting and the salute was that its right-hand side hit my own right-hand side in front and pulled me back with it. When we stopped there wasn't a piece of glass left on the right-hand side of the car, yet there wasn't a mark on the lorry.

'What do you want to do about it?' said the driver to me.

'I won't do anything about it,' I said, 'because I'm thankful to the God of Glory to be alive, and that is enough for me. I'll go into the nearest chapel to say a prayer and thank him.'

I hadn't the slightest inclination to go to court and with good reason. My car wasn't insured.

Bord na Móna's reason for sending me west was that I had my own transport and was a native speaker of Irish into the bargain. The Galwayman hadn't a word of Irish in his mouth. Our job was to look for men willing to work for Bord na Móna, and we travelled around the area, Rosmuck and Lettermore and Lettermullan and Clifden, wherever we noticed men gathered together, and the day they usually did so was dole-day. I found out that if I was dependent on them not many of them would leave Galway because they weren't at all inclined to work. There were young men there and I spoke to them in Irish. I explained clearly that they would get so much money for a day's work or else their dole would be cut off. Those were the conditions but I know that some of them said: 'To hell with them. I'm not going into any bog to kill myself.'

We had spent very little time in County Galway when we were ordered to go back to Newbridge. There were rumours going the rounds that the work which we were doing in Bord na Móna was to be cancelled and we knew then that our days were numbered. A new government had come into power. So I was out of a job again, and there was nothing for me to do but return home.

Micheál Ó Scannláin was still in Dublin and I knew that he would soon be getting his Easter holidays. I sent him word that I intended going to Graigue this particular day. He sent me back word not to leave without him, and that he would come on the bus to Newbridge and we would meet there.

On the night before leaving for home we had a bit of a get-together, just a small one in a certain house in the town. I had in my pocket two six-pound cheques that I had got from the Bord. I handed them in to the publican and he cashed them for me. I put the twelve pounds into my pocket and when it was time to go home I went over across the street to the place where I was staying, an old soldiers' barracks that Bord na Móna was renting. I headed for my room but I couldn't understand why this fellow I hardly knew was accompanying me because I was well aware where I was going and wasn't in any way confused. Stupidly enough I threw my clothes down on a chair before getting into bed. I trusted him to put out the light and go back to his own quarters. When I got up in the morning and put on my clothes all I had in my pocket was sixpence to bring me and my car to Graigue! I went searching for the fellow whom I suspected but was told that he had skedaddled off to Dublin on the bus.

Micheál came along in his own good time and I told him truthfully what had happened.

'Don't be short of money at all,' he said. 'I have some.'

And he had. We filled the car with petrol and hit the road. I was back in Graigue that evening with a car but without a job. That didn't put a stop to me, though. I used to be out early and late, coming and going in the car as I pleased. It was very noisy. My mother who had the hearing of a thieving pig used to sit in the corner with her stick. Whenever I came near Clogher on my way home she would hear the car and would announce prophetically: 'The farting car is coming.'

I didn't have the farting car very long because I hadn't the money to keep her on the road.

One Sunday evening there was a knock on the door. It opened and three men came in. They spoke in English and were looking for me. They introduced themselves. They were from near Tralee. Their leader, who was the oldest and also their spokesperson, said that they had heard that I had a car and a hound for sale, which was true, although the hound didn't belong to me. My heart jumped but I didn't let on a thing because I was worried about the money. I showed him the car and the hound and he offered me fifteen pounds which I refused. The upshot of it all was that I sold the two for twenty-five pounds but I still hadn't got the money into my hands.

We went as far as Ballyferriter. They were on their way home from Tralee but where was I going? That is a question two people couldn't answer. We went into a certain house. The two of us had a hugger-mugger, he handed over the money and we had a drink. In fact we had two drinks. I started thinking things over. Everything I had was now gone except whatever little bit of money I had in my pocket. Every time I put my hand into my pocket I would feel the money at the bottom and say to myself: 'Keep back! Keep out from the reef or the day will come when you will long for a pound and won't have it.'

After a while my three men went off to Tralee and I came back home. It was just another day. I went off to bed. In spite of my level best the money lasted no more than a week and so my finger was in my mouth again.

17
THE STONE-BAG

A few days later somebody met me and said: 'Tell me, do you know that they are looking for fellows like you in Dublin? There's a certain number of men to be taken on as postmen.'

I applied for the job and after a few days I got word to go to the big city, so off I went. I knew the road well by this time. I felt embarrassed the first day I went into the General Post Office. There was a gang of us together and whom should I notice but two or three lads who had been privates in the army when I was the big shot, as they thought. They were amazed to see that I was reduced to their own level that day. I felt somewhat ashamed and disgraced. Thank God I hadn't the name of being too strict in the army because if I had maybe I might not be here today. They soon found out that I was just like one of themselves and of course the poor creatures didn't have to call me 'Sir' as they had to do in the army. He who exalts himself shall be humbled and that was true in my case, I suppose. Talk of being noble and lowly and humble, we must do as we are told now and again, especially the day we die. When God, praise be to him forever, tells us to come we must do so, whether we are humble or noble.

We got a little training as postmen but I promise you that it wasn't a whole lot, only just enough to be able to distinguish one letter from another. We trained for some days and were then told to go our different ways, that each of us would get his own area of the city and carry out his duty carefully, but it is very hard to do it correctly the first time or even for a month or two, maybe.

The first morning I was sent out from the Pearse Street office with my bag on my back. That same bag made me feel very sad, and indeed so did the clothes that went with it. I had nice clothes on me before that in the army with lovely bright shiny buttons that would blind you on a bright sunny day. But I didn't have to take care of them. If I had they would have been neither yellow nor white but as black as soot.

In a way the postman's work was very hard. Not only did you have to be up at five o'clock in the morning but you had to be at work and have signed on by six. There was a man with a pen waiting for you, and he was anything but pleasant. If you weren't there on the stroke of six a red mark was put opposite your name. The amount of time you were late was recorded against you and taken out of your few shillings on payday. That was the first thing that disheartened me, seeing the man with the red pen having nothing else to do but keep an eye on me.

I was informed that the centre of the city around Rutland Street was to be my area. I soon got to know it. Naturally I was very slow at the start because of having to enquire where this house and that street were. After a month or two I knew the people of the area well and they knew me too. Yet I had to ask directions now and again. Quite often I didn't know where a certain house was because Dublin is a very complicated city. I found out that the people in my area were the finest and the nicest I ever met, although they were the poorest in terms of money and worldly wealth. There was a house, or maybe two or three, which vied with one another to see who would give me a cup of tea in the morning. I had no bicycle so it was easy for me to slip in and while I was in the back-kitchen with my drop of tea and a sandwich, maybe even a boiled egg, the woman of the house was at the door just in case the enemy might come around in his car. The enemy in question was one of the big shots from the Post Office. It was his job to keep an eye on the likes of me for fear that I might go trespassing. Smart and all as they were I was cute enough for them although I was often caught. I thank God that I was never charged because some of them were as bad as the Black and Tans, the crowd that went before them.

I wasn't long working there when I found out that it was in that same neighbourhood Matt Talbot lived. Matt is with the God of Glory this long time and is high up too. I was told one day where he lived. I knocked on the door. A woman opened it. I saluted her politely.

'Tell me,' I said, 'is this where he lived?'

'It is,' she said. 'Would you like to see his room?'

'I would, very much,' I said, 'and I'm very thankful to you.'

I followed her upstairs where the poor man, if you could call him poor, used to lie at night. He is a rich man now. There was nothing there but the bare bed. There wasn't even a chair. The mattress was hard. There was no bolster, no pillow. The woman told me that he used to spend his nights there, more than likely not asleep but on his two knees praying.

Shortly afterwards I was informed that if I applied I could transfer to any of the other offices around the city. The person who informed me wasn't one of the bosses because they would have left me there until I dropped dead, if I was prepared to stay. Anyhow I was told that there was a very nice area in Phibsborough, one which was much smaller than the Pearse Street area. There were about twenty postmen there, the work was easy and you could come and go as you pleased. As well as that the area wasn't as complicated as the city centre.

I will never forget until my dying day my first morning in Phibsborough. I was all set and had been directed where to go with the 'stone-bag'! The first thing I asked for was a bicycle because I had been told that I was entitled to one for the journey that lay ahead of me. There was a man outside in the yard in charge of the bicycles. I went out to him. My name was registered in Irish but instead of calling me Ó Cinnéide as was on the paper in front of him he called me 'Mister Canada' and never afterwards called me anything but 'Canada' because he was incapable of pronouncing a name like Ó Cinnéide. Being an Englishman he was as ignorant of Irish as I was of French. I asked him politely where the bicycle was. He handed it over to me. I looked at it. I felt it here and there with my hand. I shook it as you would shake an old cow that you might suspect of being in-calf.

'My God!' I said to myself, 'this wouldn't take me across the road if I jumped up on it.'

I looked at the man and said: 'Is that the bicycle I must use today?'

'That's your bicycle,' he said politely.

I looked at him again.

'It is on this my job depends!' I said. 'Well, I'll tell you one thing and one thing only. If Pádraig Pearse or De Valera himself, and I have a great regard for the two of them, were to ask me to get up on that yoke I wouldn't, and neither will I get up on it for anyone here either. If I don't get another one I'm going home.'

He didn't say a word. He knew I was in earnest. It was time for me to be. I was no child. I had my back teeth. He started searching and found another bicycle, and so I started in Phibsborough. The area wasn't at all like the city centre because it included a small rural section and I was delighted with that.

It was always my way, and it still is, to talk to everyone I meet, and that was something a postman wasn't allowed to do. We were told when being trained that we had no permission to talk except when looking for directions now and again if necessary, especially when starting off. But I didn't give a damn about that rule. I found out that there was a guard living in a certain house in the area who was from Kerry. As the old people used to say, I put talk on him. We soon got to know one another very well. I stopped to talk to him on the street one day. I remained on the bicycle with one leg on the footpath and the other on the bicycle ready to take off if I had to, but I was too late. A voice called me from the other side of the street where there was a car and a man sitting in it.

'Oh, you devil,' I said to the guard. 'I'm caught.'

I had to go across. The man in the car told me who he was. I knew I was caught red-handed when he told me he was the supervisor.

'I have three charges against you,' he said.

I nearly collapsed but the only thing was that I knew he couldn't hang me. One of the charges was that of talking to a member of the public without good reason, the second one of having a cigarette in my hand – which I had and still have – and the third that one of the buttons on my jacket was dirty. To be honest, they weren't just dirty. They were black for want of polishing.

118

A day or two later I was called to Pearse Street office where the big shot was stationed. I hope that I will not be as frightened going in to meet the God of Glory as I was going in to meet that fellow. He explained to me the charges being made against me. There was nothing I could say. It was written down in black and white. There was no need for proof because what that scamp had written on the paper was taken to be true. The big shot said that as it was my first time he would let me off, but that if it happened again I would have a different story to tell.

There was another rule that said you were not allowed to enter a house with the 'stone-bag' on your back. It was easy to enter a house when you didn't have a bicycle but if you had, and it was seen outside, the whole world would know you were there. In that case it was just a matter of waiting until you came out and then you were caught. There was a place in my area called Tolka Estate. I got to know it very well and met some fine people there. I could get tea in twenty houses in the morning, in the middle of the day and in the evening, if I had the courage to call. One day I dropped into one of the houses and, as bad luck would have it, when I came out who should be waiting for me but the fellow who gave me the bicycle on my first day in the area. He thought he had caught me out but I was learning new tricks according as I was getting that little bit older.

'I have a charge to make against you,' he said, 'that of going into a house with the postbag on your back though you know that that isn't allowed.'

'But, sir,' I said nice and gently, 'have you any idea what brought me in?'

'Oh, I haven't,' he said, 'but you went in.'

'I'll put the question to you again. Have you any idea what brought me in?'

'No,' he said.

'I'll tell you,' I said. 'I got a sudden attack of diarrhoea and what do you expect me to do, squat down in the middle of the street with the whole world looking on?'

He was left speechless. He went off and said nothing to

anybody about it or if he did I wasn't charged.

Let no one tell me that to be a postman in Dublin during the winter was a holiday. I had to go out the country at seven o'clock each morning while it was still dark, and dark for a long time afterwards. If the wind was east or north-east it was so cold that you just couldn't use your hands. All you could do was to slap them round your body. Some people still do that, especially the old, but the young people don't need to because when out in the cold weather they are equipped with gloves, something which we didn't have. My stomach was causing me problems too, and so intense was the pain on those cold mornings that I often had to throw the bicycle aside in the dark, hop in over the fence and hold my stomach. Praise be to God the pain cleared up later on and I haven't had it for quite a while now.

I became so tired of Phibsborough after a time that I asked a friend of mine if there was any chance of getting out of it. He told me that there was but I would have to think of a good excuse and put in an application. That was no problem for me.

I soon thought of an excuse and my application consisted of just four lines. Five days later wasn't I transferred to Whitehall! However it was a case of going from the frying-pan into the fire. The people in charge there were of the same calibre as those in Phibsborough. What really annoys me, when I look back on it, is that I was a native speaker of Irish, I was born in Ireland, I had spent six years in the Irish army, and now I was under the authority of those fellows who had spent most of their lives in the British army. That is what hurt me most of all but I didn't have any choice. When the old hag is hard-pressed she has to run. That was my predicament too. I had to give way.

The money which the postmen were paid at that time wouldn't raise anyone's spirits. It didn't take long to spend it. There are people in the world who can't hold on to money. I am one of them. It burns in my pocket when I have it. They say that it is easier said than gathered, and that is true. Anyhow whether I had money or not I used to go to the matches in Croke Park practically every Sunday and on summer evenings as well. This particular Sunday eight of us went there together.

After the match we dropped into a bar. The man of the house welcomed us. We went into a room where there was a circular table. We sat around the table just as if each one of us had a hundred pounds in his pocket. I know that some of us had a few shillings but there were others who hadn't.

This particular fellow ordered eight pints, one for each of us. The talk and chat started. One fellow took a swig. A second fellow did the same. We were drinking away. The amount of drink in each glass was reducing until it was about half an inch from the bottom. All of them contained exactly the same amount. The man who had ordered the eight pints got up and walked around the table. We wondered why. When he came back to his own place he pulled up his chair and sat down. Then he said, giving us a clear hint: 'It's a tight race, boys!' The money was scarce, and as well as that maybe he knew that there were two or three amongst us who hadn't the heart to part with whatever few shillings they had.

But to come back to the Post Office, the day came when I got so tired of it that I said to myself that I could stand it no longer. In the middle of the summer I wrote to my brother Séamas in America to see if he could get any work for me in that country, but he was an Irish citizen – he still is – and so he had no rights whatsoever in America except that he was earning his living there. He wrote to me saying that he couldn't do anything for me except to send me money. After a while, however, I received another letter from him saying he had come across a man who was American-born and was willing to take me on and bring me over there. I made up my mind that I would take up the offer because I would prefer to be dead than to be carrying the 'stone-bag.' I felt that there was no future for me in Ireland eager and all as I was to stay here.

Three or four months later I was all set and ready to go but I waited until the end of the year because every postman got a few shillings extra at Christmas time, not only from the Post Office for the extra work done but also from the people we used to serve, so that I nearly made as much money in one fortnight as would take me to America.

18

THE SHORES OF AMERIKAY

The day came for me to go to America. I called to the neighbours in Graigue to say goodbye. I went to Clogher and Clogherbeg because a girl from there was to travel with me, and her father gave me ten shillings out of the goodness of his heart to take care of her. But I am afraid that it was more a case of her looking after me because in those days, and also nowadays, the young people could teach the old.

I was very lonely leaving home. I was bound to be because I was leaving my parents and the spot which was dearest to my heart. Perhaps I should point out that I was thirty-eight years of age and that was too old for me or anyone else to go so far away from home. I was leaving my father and my mother behind, not to mention my brothers and sisters. Of course the old couple were the ones I felt worst about, especially my mother, because my father hadn't as much nature at all as she had. They had suffered enough from emigration since the day my eldest brother Pádraig emigrated as they never again laid eyes on him.

Anyhow myself and the girl from Clogher said goodbye to our families and went as far as Dingle. I had to call into my friends there. Tomás Callaghan was the first person I dropped in to see. I didn't delay very long because I was in a hurry. Liam Ó Lúing was the last person I visited. I told him that my one and only reason for being on the street of Dingle was to say goodbye to him. We were such close friends and so fond of each other that he cried as I left. He called me back just as I was about twenty feet from the door.

'Come here a minute,' he said to me, and gave me the last little drop of drink.

I feel sad now when I think of Liam because I never again saw him. He has gone the way of truth this long time, God be good to him.

That same evening we reached Cobh where the ship was

due to call for us the next day, but it didn't come. Around noon the day after that again we were told that the ship was leaving England and would soon arrive. The information proved correct. Its name was the *Franconia*, a fairly big ship, thirty-two thousand tons. A small boat took us out to her when she arrived in the Cobh of Cork.

We were surprised at her size and the beautiful rooms. Such was the cleanliness and luxury and style that you would be afraid to cough. There were people wearing hard caps and people wearing white coats. Everyone was told where his nest was to be that night and for the following nine nights because she was a very slow boat, and it took us more than nine days to get as far as New York.

Two days before I left Graigue I met a man on the road. He was from Clogher but was living in Ballyferriter. He was a great character.

'Tomás,' he said, 'is it true that you're setting sail the day after tomorrow?

'It is, Séamas,' I said.

'I suppose,' he said, 'that you won't be down below among the paupers at all but up above advising the captain.'

That is not what happened. It was very hard to put down the time on board, especially since we didn't have much money. Night-time was the worst part. But in a way it was a delight and a pleasure to be on board her, if only for the food alone. It was the best food I ever saw before or since and dirt cheap, I thought. I found out that there were some native speakers of Irish from Galway on board because I heard two or three of them talking in Irish. I got to know them very well but since I returned home from America I met only one of them, a chap who came to visit me when he was at home in County Meath years later. The others scattered like little birds from the nest because some of them went to New York and some to Alaska. That is the way with most of the world. We are together only a little while and then we have to scatter as sheep do when you set the dogs on them.

We were notified one day that everyone on board would have to prove that they had been inoculated against smallpox, otherwise they would have to be inoculated before landing in America. I was drawing in my horns having heard that because even though I had a paper in my pocket signed by a certain doctor – I had to give him a pound or two to do it – it was in fact a fake.

Anyhow I had to appear before the ship's doctor. He told me to take off my coat and pull up my shirt while I still pretended that I had been vaccinated. He examined me.

'You're telling lies,' he said, which was true for him because there wasn't a sign of a pin or a needle on my right hand, or on my left hand for that matter.

'All right, Doctor,' I said, 'I'll tell you the truth. I was always terrified of the needle. It frightens the living daylights out of me and that is why I am the way I am.'

But that fellow knew his job. There is nothing to it only one prick and I never felt it any more than you would feel throwing out your spit. He wasn't like the doctor I knew in Ireland who would drill four holes in your left arm, holes that would remain there even if you lived to be a hundred.

We had to call to Nova Scotia in Canada first, and may the Son of God save us, you couldn't imagine what real cold is like until you put your nose out on board ship in that place. There was nothing but snow and ice, and misery, cold and pain. It reminded me of the cold in Dublin and of the 'stone-bag'. I thought of the permanent job I had left behind me, but for me that job meant sorrow and heartbreak, not to mind my own stupidity in always staying out too late at night and then having to get up too early in the morning.

At long last we landed in New York but we had to spend a long time on board. The first people to be allowed off were the ones who as American citizens had identification papers. But the poor unfortunates like myself who were as green as grass going there and had no rights or no paper or no document that would show that we weren't just animals, had to remain back to the very end. Then there was another delay before we were allowed to go. The customs people were there with their shining clean uniforms and every one of us had to open up whatever kind of travelling bag he had and show

124

what was in it.

The man I came across was from Kilkenny.

'I suppose,' he said, 'you haven't a whole lot, or is there anything harmful in it?'

'You can open it, sir,' I said. 'You'll see that there's nothing in it only a few rags.'

That indeed was all it contained. I can guarantee you that there were no jewels or stolen goods or anything harmful except a few presents for my brother Séamas and my friends over there.

I feasted my eyes on the city of New York. It frightened the life out of me, if only because of the buildings which rose up into the sky. I couldn't understand, as I talked to myself, how anyone could have the head to go up such a height. That is the amazing thing about it. Take the Empire State Building for example. If you were at the bottom of it you would have to lie down on your back to see the top. What is the point of all this ugly treacherous carry-on? It is dangerous at the top, and in fact many is the disturbed person who went up there and committed suicide by throwing themselves down.

Oh God of bright Graces, it was a far cry from Graigue! And when I think of the madness and the savageness of New York compared with Graigue I thank God that I am back home again. The grace of God is in Graigue, there is peace of mind in Graigue, and whether a person has money or not peace is far and away better than the quarrelling and commotion which I saw in New York the very first day I went there.

I went by train from New York to Chicago, a seventeen hour journey. The train had Pullman carriages but I hadn't a hope of stretching in any one of them because you would need to have paid extra money to get a bed and go to sleep for yourself. I didn't have the money for it, and that was nothing new. I never had. I haven't had it since. I haven't got it now and I don't suppose I ever will. We must die as we are born, penniless. It doesn't matter. That will not affect our souls. Perhaps we are far better off not to have it because it often led a person astray.

I had nothing to do during the journey to Chicago but sit

down listening to other people snoring, with one eye open and one eye closed, like a hare in a bush, hoping to be told that we were near Chicago. But I am afraid that we had to be patient until daybreak and it was well into the morning when I heard the words 'We're there.'

I jumped out of my body, caught hold of the old bag and when the train stopped I got off. Cute enough I had come by a few dollars on board the ship, so I called a streetcar. The driver was a black man, a very nice and very polite fellow. I showed him the address in the city to which I was going. We got to the house and the driver charged me just one dollar. The woman of the house gave me a tremendous welcome and no wonder, because she was a cousin of mine and a very understanding woman. I stayed in her house for a fortnight until I recovered from the trip.

While I was there she and her husband were invited to a wedding one day and they brought me along with them. I had never before been at a wedding in America and I found their customs strange. You were given a small fork, a small knife and a plate, not a real plate but one you would throw away when finished with it. I don't know why they are so extravagant when they marry, and then have to look for charity later on maybe. I imagine that they spent two thousand dollars on that wedding if they spent a penny, although things were cheap then.

Anyhow as I was sticking the fork into the meat to put a bit on my plate the fork broke and the women around me started laughing.

'Oh, the poor greenhorn!' they said.

They were my own people who had arrived there maybe a year or two before me, but I was no greenhorn and I could teach them manners, manners that were taught to me by my parents and by the priests here in Ireland.

The day came for me to head for San Francisco away out west. It took us fifty-four hours to get there, more than two days and two nights. I hadn't booked a bed on the train on this occasion either. We were travelling all the time except maybe for an hour's stop now and again. The view was breathtaking as we travelled west through the Rocky Mountains which resemble a back-bone running south and north. I think the train went up to a height of seven or eight thousand feet above sea-level in places. It was wonderful to be there and to see the view, particularly at midday,with the snow and everything so white. There was no sign of the ocean, just land and mountains as far as the eye could see.

Yet I couldn't help thinking of Ireland and of Graigue. I knew that I was too old when going to America and I felt that no matter what life would hold for me in San Francisco I would never be as happy as a young person of about twenty years of age who would be full of heart starting out in life. As someone said to me before I left, I should have been coming home to Ireland with a bag of money by the time I first went to San Francisco. I was convinced that I would see my parents again. I was full of hope, I had my health, and I knew that with the grace and help of God I would get a job, which I did. The second or third time I went to America I was certain that I would come home to my parents, but on the last occasion I came home neither my father nor my mother was there to greet me. They were with the God of Glory.

We climbed to the top of the Rockies and then it was downhill west into Oakland. At that time there was a boat from Oakland to San Francisco but not now. We jumped on board the boat and soon reached our real destination, San Francisco.

I had my brother Séamas' address in my hand. I got a streetcar and showed the address to the driver who knew the area. He brought me to the house, and dropped me off. That was when the fun began because when I got to the place where my brother lived neither he nor his wife was at home and the door was locked. It was a big house divided up into three or four apartments. But on learning of my predicament the neighbours came to my aid. They brought me into their own house and gave me something to eat. Then because they knew that it was my first time there they were kind enough to bring me around the city in their car. When we got back home my brother still hadn't come, but somehow or other we tracked down the man who owned the house. He had a key to my brother's door. He opened the door, let me in and left me there. When night fell I started writing a letter home to my parents. That was, I imagine, the longest letter ever written in Irish from America to Ireland, because naturally I wouldn't dream of writing in English although that is what most of those who went to America did.

There was a man here years ago and we could be talking forever about him he was so droll, so nice, so witty. His name was Maidhc Ó Gairbhia. He heard that a certain chap from this area went to America and wrote a letter in Irish to his mother from on board ship, which indeed was true. Three or four days later the second letter arrived. This one was from New York, and was written in English. Witty Maidhc heard about it. He shook his head.

'Don't be surprised at that,' he said. 'Wasn't he in America by that time?' By this he meant that people think they must switch from their own language to English as soon as they reach America.

Late that night my brother and his wife came home. They got a real surprise. They had been expecting me for a fortnight, and were convinced that I had gone off with the wild cats, but I hadn't. I was having a grand rest for myself in Chicago, with a drop of drink under the tooth and plenty of food to eat. There was no room for me in Séamas' house that night because they were newly married and had only a small place. The three of us chatted until very near morning and then Séamas had to take me to his sister-in-law's house which was a good distance away. The house was all lit up when we got there because a daughter of the house had got married the day before. The party was on and they had no notion of going to bed as yet.

I joined them. I knew that I was welcome. A full bottle was handed to me. I accepted it willingly. I was as friendly with it as a cow with a cock of hay. I was asked umpteen questions. Everybody was surprised at how good my English was because from what they knew of my brother, who had never left Graigue until he went to America, they thought that I would have only Irish.

Next morning instead of staying in bed I got up because I

was keen to see the sights about which I had heard so much. I was so excited that I could hardly eat any food, but I guarantee you that there was nothing to wonder at after all because the sights there could not compare with the view from the Bend of Graigue back here on a fine day. I found out that my brother Pats' grave was five or six miles away and I could not rest leg or hand until Séamas took me there.

On the following day a friend brought me out to the Golden Gate Bridge. That place was a real eye-opener. Not only did I go across it but I walked part of it so that I would be able to boast about it when I got back to Ireland. I imagine that it is the nicest bridge in the world. I was amazed also at the big boats coming east from Honolulu. The likes of those boats are never seen around Ireland.

A few days later I went looking for work and got it in an oxygen plant. I don't remember anything about it now except the heat, the terrible heat and the sweat pouring down off me. The fellow who set up the plant was an old man by this time. He was from Tuam in County Galway and was rolling in money. I was introduced to him but didn't get to know him too well. I found out that he had Irish and he spoke it to me. That was a big surprise. He had been in Maynooth as a young man studying for the priesthood. He came in every morning in his Cadillac, himself and his driver, and it made me sad and heart-broken to think of my own days in the army in County Clare when I had my own car and my own driver. But it is not a case of one being noble or humble but rather of being up for a while and down for a while. Those days had passed and gone and here was I now, six thousand miles from Ireland and broken-hearted unknown to the world.

Hard and all as the day was – working there was just like being in a furnace – I always looked forward very much to the next day so as to have a few shillings of my own. Then after a month I was told that I was to be let go. I was informed that another man was looking for my job because he had been there before me. Only one of us could be kept and I was the one to be let go.

Two days afterwards I was called back again and was told

that my job would be permanent if I returned but Séamas said to me defiantly: 'Don't go back. If they let you go let them get a man in your place now. I don't want you to go back to them.'

And I didn't. I went looking for work off my own bat and put my trust in God. He never let me down and he won't let me down now either. I got a job that I would still have if I had any sense, but that is another story altogether.

This job which I got was in Gliddon's paint factory. The first thing I was taught was how to put the lid on a tin of paint. A man would fill the tin and pass it on. I was there with a bundle of lids. I would put the lid on the tin and pass it on further. There was a gadget there that took the tin and gripped it. Another gadget would come down on the tin and tighten the lid. Then the tin would go further down the line to another man, and his job was to put all the tins into a big box, glue them and put them aside. After a while I got the hang of the work. I became accustomed to it and was as good as anyone at filling a tin of paint. I was as fast as any machine, and in saying so I am not praising myself, because it was only a matter of practice and keeping your two eyes open.

That was the first real break I got in America but it wasn't great because the pay was very small.

I wasn't long in San Francisco when Séamas and his wife asked me this particular night to stay at home minding the baby, a daughter who wasn't much more than six months old. They themselves wanted to go to the pictures.

'Of course I will, and a thousand welcomes,' I said, 'but will I have much to do? Supposing she screams what am I to do?'

'If she starts grumbling and crying,' my sister-in-law said, 'more than likely it will be due to a call of nature. All you have to do is to put these clean clothes on her,' she said, showing me how to do it.

I stayed in and the baby stayed with me. She could hardly go crawling around or out on the street. During the course of the night she started. To listen to a baby just crying is fine but to have a baby screaming its head off would terrify you. I blessed myself a couple of times and asked God's help in the hope that she might calm down, but I am afraid that the screaming was only getting louder, so I started rummaging, something I had never done with any child. I nearly lost my senses when I saw the heap underneath her! I flung the dirty cloth as far away as I could and did my level best to clean the child. I found the clean napkin that had been left for me. I put the two ends together and started tightening. I caught hold of the pin and shoved it in until the child let out a screech that would startle a giant. 'Oh, God of Glory, what's wrong with you, child?' I said to her in Irish. I took off the cloth which I had just put on her and what was wrong? She was streaming blood. Obviously I had stuck the pin into her, the poor little creature. You could hear her a mile away screeching as I scratched my head through pure dint of panic. I was certain I had done the devil's own damage and that perhaps the child would be dead by the time her parents came home.

I suddenly thought of the people living across the road. Of all the religions under the sun they were Jewish, very kind and very fine people. I left the child on the flat of her back where she was, with the blood flowing from her all the time. I ran out the door and across the street and rapped on their door just as if I was being chased by a man with a gun. The woman of the house came out. I was shaking as I told her my story. She never said a word but ran back with me to look at the baby. The little creature was still hysterical.

'Calm down,' she said to me, 'it is a thing of nothing.'

She got down to work, cleaned up the blood and did a great job. I blessed myself again and thanked God that no great harm had been done and that there were such fine people as Jews still in the world. When leaving me she shook my hand and told me not to worry. She also advised me not to say anything, but hide what I had thrown away in the other rag. I followed her advice . Only for that woman I suppose I would have put the meat-knife to my throat and that both myself and the baby would have been dead by the time the people of the house came home.

19
GREAT DAY FOR THE IRISH

I was gradually getting to know the city and the people I wished to meet. Naturally I wanted to meet Irish people and I did so. I got to know Americans too of course. The Americans get on fine together. They understand one another but I and others like me who were born and bred here in the backend of Graigue could never hope to understand them. They have high notions and pretend to have a much higher standard of living than they really have. As we always said and as we still say, the most of them are full of boasting. They are not the worst, however. The poor stupid Irish people are worse and I often met a stupid Irishman pretending that he had an American accent, which he hadn't and would never have. When an Irishman is doing his best to imitate someone else he will make a mistake or let something slip in his speech to show that he is not an American.

There were other Irish people there who were so wretched that they pretended not to know their own language although they had as good a knowledge of it as I had or maybe better. It was the old weakness, the shame and the feeling of disgrace that it might be found out that you were from Ireland and had only your own language. That wasn't the case with people from other nations that I met and knew well, like the Mexicans from the south who worked with me. They certainly were proud of their own language and weren't ashamed or afraid to speak it no matter who might be listening. Of course they didn't have much English. They just had enough to get by and in any case when you are an ordinary worker you don't spend your time talking but rather doing what you are given to do. So the amount of English or any other language that was needed was very small.

St Patrick's Day is a very big day in America, especially in the large cities where all the Irish live, like New York, Chicago, Boston and San Francisco. There were many Irish people there at that time. Their descendants are still there and they are every bit as Irish as they were when I went there, and maybe forty years before that.

I remember the first St Patrick's Day parade I ever saw there. I wasn't long in America at the time, just a month I imagine. I had heard about the sights I would see but yet I never expected what in fact I did see. More than anything else I was amazed at all the green flags and the beautiful horses neatly decked out with hooves painted green. Of course that is nothing compared to the story which I heard about an Irishman who was living in a town in the eastern side of America. There was a river running down through the middle of this town, and he was so out of his mind about Ireland that he used to buy barrels of green paint and throw them into the river to make the water green.

Anyhow this particular day five of us were gathered together in a certain house celebrating and chatting and singing in Irish. We grew hungry and decided to go into an eating-house to get a meal. As it happened I hadn't a drop to drink that same day because I had promised God and man that I would give it up for a while, and I did. However three of the others in the company had been drinking and instead of following the rest of us into the eating-house they got involved with two sailors outside on the street. They got stuck in one another's throats. One of them caught one of the sailors and threw him body and soul in through the window. The glass was broken in bits.

The police came on the scene without delay, and so did others when they saw the commotion, but no one knew who had started it or what had caused it. I was there myself but if I was I had nothing to do with it. I was as innocent as the Pope of Rome.

I was trying to keep out of the way when I saw the police, or the 'cops' as the Americans call them. No wonder I was, because if you saw them coming up the street towards you your blood would quake if for no other reason than the way they walk with their forks wide apart due to the fifteen-bullet gun which they carry. Their left-hand pockets are always full of bullets in case they might use up all those in the gun.

133

I crossed the street and put my back against a wall. I was listening to the questions which the police were asking. In no time two or three of the lads were accused of starting the trouble. Then I saw one of the police heading straight for myself. He asked me if I was involved in the row. I said I wasn't, and that was true.

'Well,' he said, 'if you have any sense go home for yourself.'

'I won't sir,' I said, 'I'll go with them.'

I was afraid I might be accused of being a coward, like funky King James. I went along with them. That was Sunday. Instead of being allowed out in an hour or two, as I expected, I was kept in with the others until midday on Tuesday. We were brought before the court. The five of us were sitting on one seat, as gentle, as nice, as quiet and as frightened as a little mouse in the cat's mouth. The judge was a woman, and defending us was a black man by the name of Kennedy, a public defence counsel, as such attorneys are known.

The judge called him. When I heard the name 'Mr Kennedy' I thought she was addressing me. I stood up politely thinking that she would say to me: 'There's no charge against you. Go home.' But that is not what happened.

'Sit down, you drunkard!' she said to me straightaway.

I sat down. The evidence and the questioning started. We were doing fine until a woman stood up and said that she herself was in charge of the eating-house where we were going to have a meal and she accused us of breaking a window that cost two hundred dollars, and also that the sailor who was thrown in through it was in a serious condition in hospital. The judge hit the table with a little hammer which she had.

'Oh! This is no minor charge,' she said, 'but a serious one. Lock them up until tomorrow.'

Oh God of Bright Glory! You wouldn't believe how sad and heart-broken I became when I realised that they were putting me back in again with nothing to eat for another twenty-four hours except a bowl of porridge, the same as we had got that morning, and bread that was so stale that you wouldn't give it to the sparrows without soaking it in a drop of water.

The next day we were brought into court again. The extra charges that had been brought against us since the day before were read out. It was clear that we couldn't get off as easily as we thought. Then our attorney told us that we would need to get another attorney from outside and said that he would get one for us himself, but we would have to be held in custody until he arrived. The new attorney came at long last and had a discussion with the judge. Then he came over to us and said that we would be allowed out for a little while on condition that we came back to him a day or two later. We were quite happy with that.

When the day came we went to see him and explained our story. I was made spokesman, because I was never short of talk, I suppose. I began to speak, but the other four kept cutting across me trying to defend themselves, as if I couldn't do it properly, though the same charges were being made against me. It was agreed that we would be released this time if we swore that as long as we were in the area we wouldn't cause any more trouble. The court fined us twenty-five dollars a man. Then we asked the attorney what his own fee was. Two hundred and fifty dollars, he said, that was fifty dollars a man.

That is all the good St Patrick's Day did us, two nights in prison, two nights of sadness and worry, and costs amounting to seventy-five dollars a man.

I was so disgusted that I almost did away with myself. But I got sense, bought sense at that. I promise you I minded myself after that, and didn't go next or near those fellows again whenever they had drink taken because I must admit they were a little bit wild. I often met the likes of them before and since, yet I would never go to any trouble like I did that night because a joke often turns out to be a serious matter.

I myself rarely frequented eating-houses because the sort of fare to be had wasn't food at all. The Americans liked it, of course, because they had their own eating habits. I hated the sight of that thing called spaghetti and those hot dogs, pieces of bread with something fried in between them. You would need to be starving to eat one of them. They didn't agree with me and I never had any liking for them.

I remember I was staying one time in a lodging-house called The Wagner. It was a very strange place. There was a lot of people staying there, because everyone knows that any place where you could get lodgings for eight dollars a week was no Mark Hopkins Hotel. The floor all over the house upstairs and downstairs was lopsided and to see you walking to your room anyone would think that you were lopsided yourself.

My own room was fine and clean when I first went into it. A man from the parish of Ballyferriter brought me there in his car and you can take it from me that I didn't have much furniture. I had no contact whatsoever with the person who owned the house other than to pay the rent every Saturday.

I used to buy a bit of meat and cook it as I pleased. Good bread was available. There was no tea to be got, though, only coffee and more coffee all the time. Wherever you went you got nothing but the smell of coffee, and I never got accustomed to it. Thank God since I came home to Graigue I don't think I drank two cups of the stuff.

One day I was frying a piece of meat on the pan when there was a knock on the door. I was told that there was someone on the telephone who wished to speak to me. I ran to the telephone. It was my brother Séamas. He wanted to see me and told me to come over fast. I did nothing but ran back to my room, grabbed my coat and pulled the door out after me. But alas, the meat was frying away on the fire until the room filled up with smoke. The smoke went out under the door and out over it. Everyone in the house got the smell and they wondered where it was coming from. Thank God they found out that the destruction was taking place in my room, that the pan was burning, and the room so filled with smoke that you couldn't even stick your head in. They had to break in the door and that is the state in which I found my room when I came back the following day. As well as that I got the height of abuse from the man and woman of the house for what had happened. God knows they were dead right because they were lucky that the house wasn't burned.

When the summer came, my first one in America, I used to go out with the lads to a place called Beech Chalet. That is a football field. I don't know who owns it. Maybe the Irish own it. There was always a big crowd there with hundreds playing, and it wasn't a case of having just one football but twenty footballs if you needed them. Although I was a bit too old for the game at that time nevertheless I was still keen on it.

On one occasion a competition was arranged. If I am not mistaken there were only four teams, Cork on their own, Kerry on their own, the Province of Connacht and the Province of Ulster. The County of Kerry and the Province of Connacht were due to meet one particular Sunday. Whatever knocking about I had with the ball previously the Kerry selectors felt I was good enough to get a place on the team. I was picked amongst the forwards, where I had always played in Ireland.

The ball was thrown in, the game started and everything was going fine although I didn't get or see much of the ball. I was too old, the others were too young and too fast for me. Anyhow I went for the ball at one stage and an opponent went for me. He hit me on the head, he knocked me, he squashed me, and where did I wake up only in hospital! From that day to this I never again put on a football boot. That finished me forever with the game.

The most popular game in America is baseball. I am told that it is the most skilful game in the world but I never saw any skill in it. I never saw any sport in it either, and so I never went to watch it, just as I never went to watch a game of American football, but I saw them on television and wouldn't give my cap for them.

I thought that the antics of the baseball players on the playing field were very odd. Imagine a man lifting his leg up and lifting it a second time and a third time and then throwing the ball! You would swear to the Lord that he was trying to hit the other fellow in the eye, but of course he wasn't.

It was the queerest and the oddest game ever. It would remind you of being down on the White Strand in Clogher, getting a round slaty stone and throwing it underhand. It would skim from wave to wave, then disappear out of sight and sink to the bottom. The sort of outfit which the players wore would remind you of St Stephen's Day, the Day of the Wren, in Ireland long ago. That was especially true of the fellow whose job it was to catch the ball when it was thrown at him. He wore some kind of a mask that made it impossible to know whether he was a man or a woman, a donkey or a horse.

20

HAIGHT HIPPIES, RENO — AND BING CROSBY!

I spent a total of sixteen years in San Francisco and that isn't very long compared to the length of time which others spent there. Yet I think I got to see life in that city and especially the life of the poor, because I wanted to do so. I know that there were people born and reared in San Francisco who didn't see half the life I saw there because they didn't have to. Neither did I have to but I was so inquisitive by nature that I visited every place of any importance.

I was in San Francisco when the hippies arrived there. Neither I nor many others knew where they had come from but we had heard stories about their carry-on and how they lived.

Just for curiosity I visited them. Haight Street was the name of the street where they settled, and whatever sort of organisation they were or whatever outlook they had, what did they do after coming there but get a ladder and climb up to where the street-name was. They pulled down 'Haight' and put 'Love' in its place. Love is a great sign. That word remained there for as long as they remained, and nobody objected to it, not even the legal authorities.

They had a small shop. I can't recall what kind of knick-knacks they sold there. I went in one day. I mingled with them, not because of any pride or high notions nor a wish to fight with either my mouth or my fists, but because I wanted to find out how they lived and whether they were civilised or not. I must say that they really were civilised.

They were very shy and very secretive. Of course they were all young but to look at them you wouldn't think they were human beings at all. Both men and women were covered in down and hair and you couldn't distinguish between the two. I don't know if the women wore beards but they looked as if they did.

They never washed themselves. They never cleaned themselves. They slept on the street and in the doorways. They slept in the parks, especially in Golden Gate Park where there was plenty of room. It was easy to get in and the trees offered shelter. They slept wherever they could lie down and in that regard San Francisco was the most suitable place in America for them because the climate was so beautiful that sleeping in the open air was no problem. When I asked them once where they got a bite to eat some of them told me they didn't eat at all, and I thought that very strange because there is no one on earth who doesn't have to eat something to stay alive. The miracle is that, who ever established them, I could never figure out what their aim in life was, or why they lived such a miserable life.

The people living in Haight Street when the hippies arrived ran for their lives, especially the older ones, because they were scared stiff of appearing on the street when it was full of hippies. They all cleared off out of the place. I don't know if they sold their houses or left them after them. It doesn't matter. There wasn't a hope that they could ever again live on that street.

There were many other people, not only there but in other cities and towns around the country as well, who were oppressed and tormented by the misery of their lives. They were the poor devils who were slaves to drink. In a way they were in a worse state than the hippies, because the hippies were young, and a young person can take a lot of hardship compared to a middle-aged one. The drunks had just one rule, one of their own making. When going up and down the sidewalk collecting money for drink each went on his own. There were never two of them together in case one might get more than the other from some charitable person. They had such a craving for drink that when they had the price of one bottle they didn't wait to make the price of the second but headed for the place where the cheap wine, especially Muscatelle, was on sale. There they bought their drink and went ahide. Sometimes they might arrange to meet a companion or a friend and if they did they drank the bottle between them. Then they would arrange to meet again somewhere else after they had collected the price of the next bottle.

That was the sort of life many people in San Francisco led when I was there. I couldn't say how things are now but I suppose they are still there. God love them, when they travelled that road, the road leading to misfortune, they didn't last long because death got the better of them. It came prematurely due to weakness and hardship and misery. Nobody cared about them. Nobody knew who they were. As death approached they were brought into this big hospital where a section had been set aside for people like them. Nobody knew that they had died and it was left to the city to bury them.

I saw them after they died. A great friend of mine worked in a certain hospital in the city. He invited me to call one day and have a bite to eat with him. After we had eaten he said that he would bring me around the hospital and I would see sights. I suppose he really wanted to frighten me, but that wasn't possible, nor is it possible to frighten me now, and it never will, because I have seen too much of the world.

He brought me into this particular room. There was a table there just like that in a butcher's shop. A man was at work. There was blood on his clothes. There was blood on the table. There was blood on the floor.

My friend said to me in a whisper: 'Do you know what he's doing?'

'I haven't an idea,' I said.

'That's a human being,' he said.

'Oh God of Glory!' I said, 'are those pieces of meat a human being?'

'They are,' he said, 'that's the man's job, and a doctor will come in any minute now and it is his responsibility to find out the cause of death.'

'And Tomás,' I said to him, because his name was also Tomás, 'where will he be buried?'

'There's no need at all to bury him,' he said.

'Don't tell me that the dogs will get him,' I said.

'It doesn't matter,' he said. 'There's a special place for the likes of him. There will be neither priest nor brother nor anyone else at his funeral except those who are paid by the city to

141

bury him.'

He then brought me into another place. There was this big contraption for all the world like an oven for baking cakes or cooking meat in, just like you would have in the kitchen at home. If you opened the door what would you see! A sight that would surprise, amaze, frighten and terrify you – the two legs of a man with the soles of his feet facing you with neither shoe nor stocking on him as he lay dead on ice. According as one fellow was cut up and taken away and the doctors had found out what killed him and examined his inside, another person was brought in and the same process began all over again.

Maybe people think that I am exaggerating but I am not. I say from my heart that anyone who wants to find out whether I am lying or telling the truth has only to go there and he will be shown what I saw.

They had their own burial-place and I suppose it might well be called the paupers' graveyard. The corpses were buried by throwing them down into God's earth without flag or stone over them, without friend or companion at their funeral.

Still and all if there was poverty and misery in San Francisco there was wealth there too. If you saw some parts of it, for example the houses and the cars, not to mind anything else, you would soon realise that there was money there. And as for hotels! The Palace, I suppose, is the poshest one of them because it is the longest in existence and has a great reputation. That is where the great singer Caruso always stayed and that is where he was when San Francisco was burned in1906.

Myself and a chap from Buffalo went into a hotel once just to see the inside and find out what sort of people frequented it, but I am very sorry to have to say that I had little in common with the people there because I could hardly understand them. With their fancy clothes and their pockets of money they would frighten you even to look at them.

There was a bar in the hotel. The two of us sat down and I ordered two half-glasses of Irish whiskey which was available, but before the drinks came we wondered why we were moving and yet we didn't feel we were moving. The bar in fact was going round the very same as the world goes around with us on it and yet we don't notice. I found out later on – my friend who knew all about it told me – that it was a revolving bar.

It set me thinking what an awful pity I didn't have enough money and get permission to build such a bar back here on the top of Clogherhead. That certainly would bring people here, but I don't suppose that it will ever happen, or if it does I'll be dead and buried by then.

Nevada is to the north of California and is the only state in America that is allowed to promote gambling. There are two cities in that state which are especially famous for gambling, Las Vegas and Reno. The difference between the two cities is that all the big shots go to Las Vegas. That is where Bing Crosby and others like him used to go. That is where the money is, but I am afraid I didn't have any. Far from it.

Myself and two others decided to go to Reno for a weekend. One of the two was a man by the name of Moran – he was my ganger – and another chap named Tom Egan. We went there for the same reason as everyone else does, to bring money home.

We went there on a Saturday evening and came home the following morning. There was no question of sleep while we were there because there wasn't a bed to be got for all the gold in the world. The gambling houses are not for sleeping in but for making money with every sort of a game under the sun to coax you to part with your money, and music, music, music all the time. To go into Reno and listen to the music coming out of every single house there you would swear that there was no such thing as death in the world, that nobody ever died and no one ever would die.

The law of the state allows the bars to be open at all times. They never shut at all. They are swept and cleaned even while the people are drinking, from two o'clock in the day until two in the morning, from two in the morning until two the next day. You might think that the people were there to enjoy themselves but it is no enjoyment for anyone except for those who own the gambling houses. You can be absolutely certain that every one of them is rolling in money. Yet even they must die and what good is it to them then because there is no pocket in a shroud.

The three of us were going from house to house trying to make a few dollars. We arranged to meet somewhere every now and again because I had never been there before and was afraid that I might lose the other two and have to thumb my way home to be in time for work on Monday morning. I can't say how much they had in their pockets going there but I know that I myself had two hundred dollars. I thought that I would do the devil and all and come home with a fortune. I am afraid I came home as poor as Neáid, whoever Neáid was, and so did the other two as well.

Anyone who might ask my advice and go to Reno to see the place is in for a real shock, but I would strongly advise him not to have as much as one penny in his pocket because even if he had a million pounds going there he would have nothing a couple of days later.

When I was in Wilton I got to know a very nice chap from Limerick and we became very friendly. He invited me to his house a couple of times and I met his parents. He had a sister and you would have to look at her a second time she was so beautiful. The only problem was that she was a little bit too young for me to ask her if she would like us both to be buried in the same graveyard.

Anyhow many years later when I was in San Francisco I paid a couple of visits to Burlingame where cousins of mine lived. By a stroke of luck I found out that the girl from Limerick was living in the same town and knew my cousins. We met one day. My heart jumped and so did hers. We arranged to meet again, and we did so frequently. Sometimes she came up to me, other times I went down to her. This particular night I met her down at her place.

'I've great news for you, Tomás,' she said to me.

'What is it?' I said.

'There's a man here,' she said, 'who is very rich and is known all over the world. He has a house in this place although he doesn't live here all the year round.'

'Who is he?' I said.

'Bing Crosby, the famous singer,' she said, 'and he is going to have a big night next week. I'll be there myself and I'll arrange for you to be there too. We'll have a great night's fun.'

I nearly collapsed when I heard that I was going to Bing's house. Somehow or other this girl had got to know him very well. I don't think she was working for Bing. Of course he had Irish blood in him.

Around that time I had a friend in San Francisco who was just as big a tramp as myself. He wasn't staying with me but if the poor man found himself without a place to stretch his bones any night I would invite him to come home with me. The night before I was due to go down to Bing's house the two of us had taken a few drinks and I brought him back to my place. The bed I had was so narrow that a worm could hardly fit in it, but I had room enough in it by lying on my side. There wasn't a hope that you could stretch on the flat of your back in it because you would fall out in no time. I made a bargain with him that he could have the bed and I would go underneath on the floor. I warned him not to be tossing around in it, otherwise he would fall down on top of me. I was as happy as the King of England's son underneath and slept fine. Fairly late in the morning while the two of us were still dead asleep there was a loud knock on the door. I didn't take any notice of it and I don't know if my friend was awake or asleep or having a nightmare. The knock came again and again. Finally I shouted out loud in English who was there. The door opened slightly. I poked my head out over the clothes. There were two girls standing outside, the girl from Limerick and a friend of hers, I presume. She saw me. She recognised me and I guarantee you that it wasn't because of my good looks. As soon as she saw the get-up of me and where I was stretched after the night she did nothing but shut the door. She ran off and I suppose she is still running as a result of what she saw. She never brought me to Bing's house, and I don't blame her.

21
BLACK AND WHITE

I was working away in Gliddon's Paint Factory. Naturally enough with the coming of summer there was a greater demand for paint than there had been in the winter, and that meant extra work. We used to get two hours extra a day and, of course, extra pay to match it.

My foreman was a Mexican and you can take it from me that he was a bad egg. I couldn't understand his awful attitude. Whatever he had against me I noticed that he didn't think much of either myself or my work. Practically every day there was extra work and extra money to be got yet he never gave me the nod when the time came to go home. He never put any extra work in my way. He would let me go and keep back his own pals, that was until I plucked up enough courage to tell him when I arrived one morning that I wouldn't start work until the manager came and I could ask him why I wasn't being considered.

The Mexican told me to start work or otherwise I would hear all about it. I refused and I paced up and down the factory floor while everyone around me was working. There was I doing nothing, just looking at them. I was full of anger and bad feeling towards the fellow who I felt had wronged me.

At last the manager arrived. Instead of faulting me he praised me and said that I wouldn't be short of work as long as it lasted. From that day to the day I left Gliddon's the ganger never said as much as 'The pooka is coming' to me. He was afraid of his life of me.

Some time afterwards he was demoted, another man was put in his place, and believe it or not I was promoted. I was made night-foreman. I had been two years there by the time I got the promotion and the extra pay that went with it.

I was doing fine and was pleased with life. Yet I was always thinking of home and of going to see my parents. 'I'm going east and my love is going west' as the man said long ago.

But my love was in the east because America is to the west. My heart was in Graigue but to come home one would need a few pennies to toss around. However I had been putting a bit of money by every fortnight when I got my pay. So when the bee stung me to make the journey home I had sufficient money to bring me there and back.

I had another reason for coming home that year, 1955, because *Brú na Gráige* was to be officially opened on the last day of July. I got three months' holidays from Gliddon's although I had only spent two years with them. I came home by plane and just as we were in sight of the Blasket Island on our way from the west the hostess said: 'Ladies and gentlemen, now that we are approaching Ireland please fasten your seat belts.'

Instead of obeying her and tightening the belt around my belly what did I do? I stood up with a bottle in my hand and started singing 'Westering Home' in Irish! She came up to me and told me to have sense. I had sense. I sat down, but I don't know if I fastened my belt or not because with or without a belt I couldn't swim, and if the plane fell into the sea within four feet of Shannon Airport I would have gone straight down to the bottom. Thank God we landed safely.

Some friends of mine were waiting for me there because I had written to them beforehand. We came home to Graigue and instead of having one bottle of the hot drop – and it wasn't tea – I had six, and also an eight-gallon barrel of porter which was delivered to me at the house by order. My family thought that I was loaded with money, which I wasn't.

That was the first time I saw the new house which my parents had built. The barrel was left above in the old house but the bottles of whiskey were kept in the new one just in case.

The neighbours arrived in twos and threes. The bottles weren't long open when my father started to sing. He had old songs of his own from the Parish O' Moore, his native place. Between songs and drink and everything else we had a night to beat all nights.

On my return to America I was getting on fine in Gliddon's factory until I learned the trick of going over the fence to have a quick nip instead of staying and minding my job. I started going to the 'well' even during the night, and perhaps I used to spend too much time there. Then someone gave the game away and that put paid to me. I lost the standing and rank which I had acquired. I was demoted, but still and all I was retained and was put on day-work. The demotion broke my heart.

Sense doesn't come before age, they say, but that is the way with the human being and there is no knowing who has sense. Still it was high time for me to have sense because of my age and also because of the opportunity I had got to make a fine living and maybe gain further promotion. I will never forgive myself for the wrong I did both myself and the people who promoted me by not minding my job and showing them that I was thankful.

When a goat comes into the church it doesn't stop until it reaches the altar. I had acted like the goat.

In the end I had to leave Gliddon's, the place where I had such a great life, and endure poverty for a while. The only good thing that happened was that I got word from a friend of mine about a vacancy in the City Library. He told me to apply fast, which I did.

I headed off down to the library and went upstairs to the office where I was received kindly. The people there were extremely nice. They were delighted to hear that I was from Ireland and I went so far as to tell them that I could speak my own language and if they had any books in Irish in which people might be interested I could advise them. They were in fact delighted that someone like me had applied for the job. However I am afraid that the work I was given had nothing to do with books but rather with a sweeping brush, because that was what was handed to me the very first day I went to work, and the whole world knows that a brush isn't for writing.

At first I thought that I would be reasonably happy in the job but however much I hated the work I had been doing as a postman in Dublin I hated this job even more after a while. I had to be at work at six o'clock in the morning in Dublin but here in the library I had to start at five o'clock so as to have the place ready for people when they came in looking for or reading books. I am afraid that I was never a lover of early rising.

In spite of all that I was working away and doing well, but I was mad for fun and loved meeting the lads at night and staying out with them. The law there was that the bars didn't close until a quarter past two in the morning. I was often out until that hour and yet a thought would come into the back of my head and I would ask myself: 'Tomás, how will you get up at half past four to go to work at five?'

So far so good. This particular morning – I must admit that we had great sport the night before – I was at work at five like everybody else. I went about my task having been told that there was a sitting-room up on the fourth floor which needed to be swept.

I took my brush with me and went up into the room. The first thing I noticed was a fine soft seat about six feet long on which the big noises who used to visit the library sat and were wined and dined. The devil tempted me so I sat down in the middle of the floor with my brush in front of me, and I imagine that I said to myself: 'Isn't that a horrible implement?'

I wasn't long sitting there when I began to doze off, and again the devil tempted me so I stretched out full length and breadth on the seat. The minute I did so I fell dead asleep. Very soon someone gave me a prod and shook me. I let a roar out of me and opened my eyes.

'Get up,' said the man, 'and go downstairs. Put on the clothes you were wearing coming in and go home.'

That was it. Instead of going to work at six o'clock in Dublin I was sent home from work at six o'clock in San Francisco. Anyhow I went home with heavy feet and my head under me, and with good reason because I would have no income until I got the next job wherever that might be.

Soon afterwards I met a man who was kind of important and told him what happened, that it was my own fault, that I got tired and fell asleep and that there was nothing else that I could be accused of. He did me a favour. He went to the head of the library and as a result I was taken back for the second time. It was all to no effect though, because I lost the job again and it doesn't matter why. I am too ashamed to put it on paper. It is not that I stole anything. Thank God I can't be accused of that.

Job or no job I went out with my friends every night. The place most frequented by Irish folk was the premises of the KRB, as we used to call it, that is the Knights of the Red Branch in Market Street which is the biggest street in San Francisco.

It had two floors, upstairs and downstairs. There was always Irish music and Irish dancing there. Maybe the foxtrot was there too, but my dancing days were over. I was just about forty and dancing was far from my mind. Twenty years growing, they say, twenty years in bloom, twenty years fading and twenty years when it makes no difference whether you're alive or dead. So I was fading and neither dances nor any sport of that kind worried me but rather the fact that I was six thousand miles from my parents and my native place. The loneliness and depression affected me all the time, and so I was often nearer to the counter and to the drink than I was to the dance floor.

As you can imagine we Irish clung very much to one another. I was usually in the company of the native speakers of Irish, especially the Connemara people and the few who were there from West Kerry. We never spoke anything but our own language and that wasn't because of any grudge or hatred of anyone who might be listening to us. It was just that we preferred Irish to English because it was the language in which we were most fluent. As everyone knows there is a slight difference between Munster Irish and Connacht Irish but with a little bit of practice we got over that problem. My brother Séamas was usually with us too because he was dead keen on Irish and he helped me a great deal to understand the Connachtmen in the beginning.

There were a few Irish people who were very bitter and nasty to me and said that it was bad manners on my part to speak Irish where there were people who didn't know it. There was one fellow who used to say to me: 'In the name of heavens, wouldn't you speak English so that we could understand you?'

I told him plain and straight that the Spaniards, the Italians, the Germans, the Chinese and all the other races there were proud of their own languages, and that they spoke them without any apologies to anyone, and didn't give a hoot about the Americans or anybody else. Some of the Irish were very faithful to their language and were thinking night and day of their own country and of their own people. I am sorry to have to say, though, that there were others who said straight from the heart that they didn't care if they never again laid eyes on Ireland or never set foot on their native heath, and they proved it too. They had the money to come on holidays but would not do so because they had some sort of hatred and grudge against Ireland on account of having had to go to America to earn a living.

The same was true of the people of Irish blood who were born in America. You would be surprised how faithful many of them were to this country and how they looked forward to the day that they would have enough money to come here. There were others, even my own aunt's family, and it never entered their minds to come. Ireland meant nothing to them.

The Irish weren't the only people with whom I mixed in America. I got to some know black people very well too. For one thing some of them worked with me, and as well as that when at one stage I was finding it hard to get lodgings I got a place in Scott Street. I was surrounded there by black people. They were under me, above me, east of me and west of me. If you went out into the street and looked around you wouldn't see as much as one white face. I had given up the drink at the time. I can't say now how I got to know some of them but they used to hold meetings from time to time and I got an invitation to those meetings. I was the only white person present but maybe they were whiter than myself in their hearts. They were fine people and I am certain sure that they wouldn't hurt or harm anyone.

There were other black people, though, and they were a bad lot. I remember I was working in a bar once. It wasn't much of a job, just cleaning out the premises after closing time every night, and it was always three or four o'clock in the morning by the time I left for home.

This particular morning I was within two hundred yards of where I was staying when I felt that someone was following me. There wasn't another living soul on the street, just the two of us. I heard the footsteps as he gained on me and then he said: 'Your money or the knife!'

I ran screaming. It was the luck of God that there was a car passing by at the next corner. I ran out into the middle of the street in front of it. I put up my hand to stop it. Who should be in the car only two white people!

They guessed straightaway what was wrong as they had seen the black man running off around the corner.

'Hold on there,' said one of the men, 'until we come back again to you.'

They followed him around the block. After a little while they came back to me.

'Go home now,' they said to me. 'The way is clear.'

I went home. Just as I was near the door of my house another black man came after me saying the very same thing, that he would shoot me if I didn't give him my money. He didn't catch up with me, however, because I made a bolt for it. I was too fast for him although I was over forty years at the time. Quite a lot of the houses in San Francisco have stairs on the outside and so had my lodgings.

I ran up the stairs. It was the will of God that I had the key in my hand. As I was pushing it into the keyhole knowing I was safe I shouted some insulting remarks down to him. But if I did I was sorry afterwards because that fellow might keep an eye out for me and who was to know, he might do the job properly the next time and hit me down on the top of the head and kill me all because of the few dollars in my pocket. The likes of him wouldn't think twice about it. That sort of thing happened very often because there were very many black people who had no work and the white people had no time for them. On the other hand they were reputed to be very lazy.

One of them – we called him 'Smithy' – worked with me for a while. He was a straight kind honest fellow. He was very religious too. We got to know one another so well that he invited me to dinner one day. He spoke in a whisper in case the other workers might find out about it because there was no black man in the factory other than himself. I gladly accepted the invitation, although when I mentioned it to friends of mine they told me to have nothing to do with him and steer clear of him, but I had my own ideas, and I still have about lots of things. He called for me. I was ready for him, all dolled up in a fine suit of clothes and looking like a gentleman. We went to his house and he introduced me to his wife. Of course she wasn't white either but as black as coal.

Smithy was a Baptist and his main purpose in inviting me was to compare his own religion with mine. I brought my Bible with me, one I had got some time before that for a quarter of a dollar in a secondhand bookshop. Smithy believed in the God of Glory, in heaven and in hell just as firmly as does the Pope of Rome. I said to him: 'Whisper, Smithy, how could there be any difference between us since we have the same aim and purpose, that is to get to God's heaven?'

His wife was very shy and so she didn't take any part in the discussion. She just sat down at the table with us while we were eating, but I think she was watching me out under her eyelashes for fear of the worst, because more than likely she was never before in the company of a fellow like me. If Smithy kept on trying until the western world fell on the eastern world to persuade me that he himself had the true religion he could not make me budge from the religion in which I was baptised. Bad and all as I am I will hold on to it. I couldn't make Smithy budge either, nor did I try, because I honestly feel that a person should stick to what his mother tells him when he is on her knee.

It made no difference. We were as friendly as ever and I do not regret that I accepted the invitation. It is a long time since I saw Smithy, and I will hardly ever again see him in this life. I don't know if he is dead or alive but I often think of him.

22
THE NATURE OF THE SALMON

There was a time – it wasn't the only time – when things were
going very much against me. I had no work and I was con-
centrating too much on the bottle. Somehow or other I found
out that there was a certain place where the likes of me could
get shelter and lodgings until they recovered. This house was
in Haight Street, the very same street where the hippies came
first day. The house was called Ten Thirty-Five because that
was its number and it was written in great big letters on the
outside. A blind man without eyes could see it. I headed for the
house. Sheehy was the name of the man in charge, and his
great-grandfather was from Ireland. He was an awkward cus-
tomer and would frighten you even to look at him, not to mind
the way he spoke. Still and all he took me in. The house was
divided in two with the women in one part and the men in the
other. It was said by some people that the men and women
used to occupy the same quarters but that was not so because
Sheehy wouldn't allow it. He was a Catholic and a man of great
faith. The people in the house, both men and women, were very
like myself in that they were all unfortunate creatures who
came from good people but had fallen by the wayside because
of the drink. Whoever started the work done by that house did
a great lot of good for many people, although there were others
for whom it did very little because nothing could put them
back on the right road.

Sheehy himself had spent a good part of his life in misery
before he recovered and was given the honour of being put in
charge of the house. He was middle-aged at that time. He spent
all his time on the job and went out only very rarely. He was
on watch at the door every night in case anyone, man or
woman, came in drunk. He had one rule, a good one too. Anyone whom Sheehy caught coming in smelling of drink was
given the road there and then. In a way Sheehy showed little
pity or compassion. It was just a case of 'Go up to your room,

gather up your rags and get out.' I myself saw him doing it to people, and upon my soul you couldn't but pity a poor wretch who was put out in the middle of the night, knowing that he had neither house nor home to go to, and maybe nothing in his pocket that would enable him to get a bed elsewhere. Still Sheehy was more or less right because he had to keep order. Thank God I wasn't long in Ten Thirty-Five when I pulled myself together and got work in the kitchen there. I was getting twenty dollars a week and because I wasn't spending the twenty dollars I was putting money away. For nine months I was conducting myself properly and if I had spent nine years there I suppose I would really have been on the pig's back.

I'll never forget one man who was there during my time. He was a pleasant fellow and well-educated. He worked as a postman in the city of San Francisco. Every morning when leaving the post-office he would sling the bag, packed tight with letters, up on his back. He covered only one building because that building, with its rooms and offices, was so big that it used to take him the whole day to deliver the mail there. He never delivered letters to any other house. The work was very hard, and what really killed him was the stairs that went up and up from floor to floor. It is safe to assume that the poor man must have been sad and broken-hearted because what did he do in the end? He put a knife to his throat. God rest him, I cried when I heard the news.

I settled down to work again in America but couldn't put Graigue out of my head no matter how hard I tried. So I made up my mind to come back again to the old sod as soon as I had enough money to bring me there. Two years later I had saved the fare and I got permission from the company for which I worked to go home. The excuse I gave them was that my parents weren't well. Maybe that wasn't entirely true because although my mother wasn't well my father had never been better.

I came to Ireland by air and walked in home on Christmas Eve Night, of all nights. They weren't expecting me and that was all the better. One thing that upset me, though, and it still upsets me, was that my poor mother didn't recognise me at all.

It was clear that she was failing and she lasted only a year after that.

I was always a rover and a couple of days after Christmas the bee stung me again. I had a rented car and myself and a friend decided to go on a trip to County Meath where the parents of the Ó Cualáin boys, my friends back in San Francisco, lived. The old couple were there to meet us. The old man was within a year or two of the hundred and I remember him well sitting on a chair in the corner while I was on my two knees beside him plying him with a drop of whiskey. We had whiskey and poteen and went down a good way in the bottles. When it was time for us to be going I felt in great fettle, so I thought, and no wonder after all I had drunk. As we were going through Dublin on our way home I scratched a car that was parked on the side of the street. If I had the same scratch on the tip of my tongue I wouldn't even notice it, so we continued without saying a thing to anyone.

After spending a few days in Graigue we set off again. On this occasion we were bound for Kilrush in County Clare to see the Crottys, my old friends since the time of the army. The woman of the house was one of the best women ever to break bread. She was full of music, fun and heart. Even though it was in the depth of winter and no place looked its best we paid a flying visit back to Kilkee one evening. We hadn't gone very far when we spotted a guard on the road ahead of us. As we approached he put up a paw that was as big as a dish. I stopped. I put my head out the window.

'You're in a hell of a hurry,' was the first salute he had for me, and it wasn't in Irish. I wondered why he should say such a thing. I asked him cheekily what was bothering him.

'I'll tell you,' he said. 'There's a charge against you and we have been looking for you all over Ireland for the last three weeks, but we now have you.'

'What have I done out of the way?' I said in all innocence.

'Well now,' he said, 'you hit a car in Dublin and you didn't stop.'

That really knocked the heart out of me because I knew I was guilty and was now trapped. He asked me if I had my insurance certificate with me and I told him I hadn't, that the car I had was rented but that I had a driving licence all right. He wrote my name and address in a small notebook.

'When you get back to Dingle, and go there straightaway, call into the guards and they will tell you the whole story.'

From that day to this I could never understand why the likes of me could be a worry to the guards of Ireland, yet I was, because I found out later from a guard that my name was in every barracks in the twenty-six counties. You would swear that I intended killing someone, or worse still that I already had killed someone.

When we got as far as Dingle the guards told me that I would have to appear before the court in Dublin two days later. It was no time for delay. I paid a quick visit home to Graigue, started getting ready to leave, and said goodbye to my parents. To make a long story short when I should have been before the court in Dublin I was six thousand miles away over in San Francisco. That was the beginning of the year 1958.

Even if I were to travel the whole world one of the finest people I could hope to meet was a chap by the name of Vince Newell, God rest him. If anyone has gone to Heaven he has. I was staying in a house in San Francisco that wasn't in very good condition and I have a feeling that I wasn't paying a penny for it. There were two people living there. They weren't married but were related in some way or another. When I went there first I was in reasonably good health. I was working and paying my rent but when my health failed the money failed too. Still they allowed me to stay there and I will always be grateful to them for that.

I got to know Vince Newell while I was staying with them. He was working in a bar a short distance away. He was very fond of me, why I don't know. He knew that my health had failed and that I wasn't earning any money. I was in my room one morning when there was a knock on the door. The woman of the house told me that a man at the bottom of the stairs wished to talk to me. I went down. Who was there but Vince!

'Tomás,' he said to me straightaway, 'whatever duds you have now, gather them up and throw them into the car, but be quick because I'm in a hurry.'

I stood there goggle-eyed, because I never expected anything like that. I was sitting in the car having thrown my few odds and ends into the back when I asked him what he intended doing with me, throw me into the harbour or what.

'I'll tell you later on,' he said.

Off he drove across the city and never stopped even once until he pulled up outside the door of his own house. It was a new house and he himself was newly married. He brought me into a room so posh that you would be ashamed to put a foot in it if you had any dirt on the sole of your shoe.

'Tomás,' he said to me all of a sudden, 'this is your room now and for as long as I know you that's where you'll be.'

And that is where I was until misfortune struck me once again.

I had nothing to do except eat three meals a day, shave myself and go out and come back when I pleased. I didn't have to pay any rent nor was there any mention whatsoever of it, and what surprises me most of all is why did Vince do me such a good turn since I wasn't related or connected to him in any way. He worked in the bar in the city from six o'clock in the evening until two o'clock in the morning and I used to go there with him. I was drinking then, if I could get drink, and very often I couldn't. I used to pass the night going from bar to bar to meet Irish people whom I knew. This particular night, when I was in a bar a short distance from the one where Vince worked, a man came in and tapped me on the shoulder.

'You won't believe who's dead,' he said, 'your friend Vince Newell.'

I don't know how I didn't fall down in a weakness and stay there.

'Come along and you'll see,' he said.

We went down to the bar. It was locked. I saw the cops inside. I saw a priest there also and then I realised that my friend was telling the truth. I started crying and cried my fill. From that night on I didn't go next or near the house as much as once because the loneliness and the heartbreak wouldn't let me do so. How could I face his widow or what could I say to the poor creature? Whatever odds and ends I had there I left them there. There was nothing valuable amongst them and even if there was I couldn't care less. If I was as rich as Damer or as poor as Neáid I couldn't go back for them. One thing which I know I left there, because I was always very fond of it, was a statue of St Anthony that I had bought some time previously.

I had to go looking for lodgings again. I found a room but take it from me that it wasn't one that you would put a bishop into. The bed was no great shakes nor the bedclothes either, but they were good enough for me. Every morning when getting up, there and in many other places as well, I had the habit of kicking the clothes down with my feet, and when I came in at night to go to bed I would pull them back up again. That is how I dressed my bed for many a long day, and yet I used to sleep like a stone.

I was out one night with the lads carousing and having a good time, and was very late getting back to the house. I went upstairs. I was just taking the key of the room out of my pocket when I spotted two locks on the door, one above and one below, and if I was as tall or as well-built as Jack Dempsey I couldn't reach the one on top. Even if I could I hadn't any key to open it or indeed the lower one either. I realised straight-away what had happened. I hadn't paid the rent.

All of a sudden the thought struck me that there was no hope of getting in that night at any rate, wherever I might spend it. I thought of my great friend Tommy Ó Sé from Caher-atrant in the parish of Ventry. He was living not too far away from me. I rushed over to his house before he would have gone to bed. I knocked on the door and this person opened it. I asked if Tommy was in. I was told that he was. He came out to me in no time with a smile on his face.

'What's troubling you, Tomás?' he said. 'Are you running from the cops?'

'Damned near it, Tommy,' I said, telling him my story.

'Don't worry,' he said, going off down the stairs with me.

We soon got to the house where I had my room. Tommy knocked and the woman of the house put her head out.

'Tell me,' said Tommy, 'is it true that you've thrown out

my friend?'

'It is,' she said, 'because he didn't pay the rent.'

'Have you anything else against him,' he said, 'except that the rent is unpaid?'

'Isn't that enough?' she said. 'Isn't that why I'm here?'

'How much do you want?' said Tommy.

She mentioned the amount in question. I can't remember now how much.

Tommy did nothing but put his hand in his pocket and handed her the money.

'Remove the two locks from the door now, if you please,' he said.

She went back into the house, got the two keys, took off the two locks and the criminal was allowed in.

I'll never forget the goodness of the wonderful people whom I met in America and who were so generous with their help when I was straddled with misfortune. Vince Newell and Tommy Ó Sé were two of them.

The years were slipping by and life wasn't getting any better for me. Not at all. It was the very opposite. It is no lie to say that I was living a life of misery and there is no point in describing it here now. To cap it all my health was failing and the rheumatics were setting in. That meant I wasn't able to do much work. In the end I had to go into a state hospital in the town of Ukiah in Northern California.

That hospital was like a town. It was divided up into sections and there was every kind of person under the sun there. There were black people and yellow people and white people and no group had any connection with the others. There were people there who had been destroyed by drink and were trying to recover. I myself was one of them. Some of them never went to bed at all because they were too disturbed.

There were hippies there too, real hippies. Some of them would frighten you, the men with beards and long hair, and the women with their heads shaved. But that was the way they wanted it, and everyone must be allowed to do as he pleases. And such music as they had! It never stopped at any time of the day or night, and you would pity the sick people who had their own complaints and were trying to sleep.

I was recovering gradually and after a certain amount of time I got a little job, if you could call it a job, in the canteen. It consisted of bringing the daily papers around on a bicycle to those patients and workers who wanted them. I was living away like that from day to day and from month to month. I was all the time thinking and wondering whether I should stay over there or come back home to Ireland. I had plenty of good friends there and wouldn't go hungry or thirsty, but my own people would be better to me than all the friends, no matter how good they might be. Still if I came home twenty-one times and had no prospects other than gazing around me there was no chance that I could survive. I would need to have an income of some sort and I couldn't do any real work because my health wasn't up to it. So I had no other choice but to stay where I was and put my will with God's will. He didn't let me down.

One day a doctor who was working in the hospital came to see me. There was a social worker with him. Neither of the two was a Catholic and maybe it was just as well. The reason they wished to see me was to enquire if I would like to return to Ireland. I told them that I would love to but that there was the problem of money.

'Your health has failed,' they told me, 'and so it is our opinion that if you go home you will be entitled to a certain amount of money from the state. After all isn't that why you were paying money to the state while in employment?'

The three of us put our heads together and the end of the story was that they sent off an application signed by me. Some time later I got word that a referee from Washington DC would call to me on a particular day. The appointed day came and myself and the doctor appeared before the referee. He had a girl with him as secretary and every word that came out of the mouths of the various speakers, myself included, she recorded it on tape. The last question the referee put to the doctor was: 'Doctor,' he said, 'is it your opinion that this man is so sick that he is unable to work?'

'I have been a doctor for a long time,' he said, 'and it is my firm belief, and from my heart I say it, that he is not able to do any day's work, and will not be, because of his complaint.'

'That is all I need,' said the other man.

Everybody shook hands. I went off out with my head under me. The other three remained. It wasn't long until I was called back in again.

'Tomás,' said the doctor to me as he shook my hand, 'I think we have won the day, and with God's help it won't be long until you hear the good news, as sure as your name is Tomás.'

My heart leaped and I suppose, if I had money in my pocket just then and if there was a 'well' near me, that through pure dint of joy I would have drunk enough to kill me. Not very long afterwards a letter came saying that my application was successful, that my few shillings would come, and I could do whatever I wanted with them wherever I wanted. I thanked God, asked him for his help to bring me home safely, and promised that if he did I would never again look west towards America. It wasn't that I was ungrateful to America because America had been good to me, and still is, but even the very bird prefers the area where it was hatched.

As soon as ever I had settled everything I said goodbye to California. I sent word to a friend of mine in Boston that I would be landing at the airport there. He was there to meet me on the dot. We had a couple of hours together before an announcement was made that it was time for the passengers for Ireland to board the plane. When I saw the name St Brendan on its outside I knew that I would soon be home. I went on board, the plane took off and I have never since laid eyes on America.

I was back home again in Ireland on the fifth day of June 1969. On my way west from Shannon I thought of the salmon that is spawned north in the River Feoghanagh and goes as far west as the coast of Canada. When that same salmon is preparing to spawn it comes east again to the River Feoghanagh to the very same place where itself was spawned. That is the nature of the salmon. That was my nature too.

When I got to Graigue my heart opened up with joy as I

looked out at the sea, at Sybil Head and the rocks that I knew so well ever since I came into this sinful world. It seemed to me that they had never looked as beautiful. There was a big change at home, however. Since I left the house thirty-six years previously many is the day and night I came home sometimes early, sometimes late, to find my parents before me, but this time they were missing. The Lord had called them.

I realised that as things were I would find it hard to kill the time. Every day I used to gaze out to sea and think of the old people who spent their lives struggling against it in an effort to make a living, but there was a special charm about it now because the weather was beautiful. I had a few pounds in my pocket after coming from America and it struck me that the best thing I could do was to have a currach made for myself. I was not contemplating any great rowing feats, only just that it would provide me with a pastime, and I could go fishing for pollack or mackerel when the fine day came. It was built down in Letteragh and having brought it home I put it on a stand in Bealbawn.

Anyone looking at me would take me to be a fisherman but God help the household that depended on me and my little currach to keep them supplied with fish because the amount of fishing I ever did was negligible, the sort that those people do who go out from the pier and when the first breeze of wind comes they scurry home. I had no notion at all of going out as far as the Light as did the generation that went before me.

I remember cycling one day to Bealbawn. I was completely on my own. I called up to my first cousin Seán Ó Cinnéide in Smerwick, God be good to him, to see if he felt like going out fishing. He told me that he couldn't do so because he had other jobs to attend to at home, but he would put the currach afloat for me, which he did. I set off for the mouth of the harbour armed with pollack gear and, of course, an anchor-stone. The weather was beautiful and I spent most of the day on the sea even though there wasn't much fish coming my way.

When I decided to go home I pulled in my line, put out my two oars as any seafarer might do, and headed for the pier. If

God were to break my heart I got the feeling that I was making no headway whatsoever and I was wondering what on God's earth was wrong with me, considering all the notions I had of myself as an oarsman. At long last I found out my mistake. Wasn't the anchor-stone resting on the bottom of the sea all the time and the rope tied to the stern of the currach! A man threw it in my teeth afterwards.

'You are the one,' he said, 'who's bragging about being a fisherman and there you were pulling a big stone around the sea after you!'

I went out fishing for pollack another day accompanied by two locals. I was on the lines and they were rowing. All of a sudden a fish bit. I hauled it in and cast out again fast. No sooner had I the feathers in the water than I caught four pollack all at once. I knew then that the conditions were right and that it would be a good idea to have a second person fishing.

I threw a line to the man nearest me but as I was handing it over one of the hooks got caught in my finger. The hook was tied to the line and I was doing my level best trying to pull it out but there wasn't a hope because the barb had entered the flesh. The barb is the hook which holds the fish when it bites. There was nothing for it but to cut the line with my teeth, leave the hook stuck in my finger and come home. It was the will of God that there was a car going to Dingle just after we came home, and it brought me to the doctor. He gave me the needle twice and that put me to sleep, I guarantee you. He did the job. He took out the hook and I had to pay him a pound, would you believe! I went into Tom Long's pub before leaving Dingle and spent another two pounds there, not on doctors but on myself. That was the costly fishing for me.

Though I lost a little bit of money on that visit to Tom Long's I thought that I would make a fortune another day I was there. I was sitting down as comfortable as could be, my two feet up on a chair, people all around me, everything to my satisfaction and not a poor person among my relations, so I thought. The next thing was that the man of the house came over to me and asked me in a whisper if I would like to have my picture drawn.

'Who wants to do it?' I asked.

'Look at him over there,' he said. 'He's not Irish but that doesn't matter. If you agree I'll get a copy of the picture and you'll get another one yourself.'

I felt very important altogether.

'Will I get anything out of it?' I said innocently.

'You will,' he said jokingly. 'You might get five hundred pounds.'

'Many thanks be to God,' I said. 'The day has come for me to make my fortune. Whoever he is tell him I'm agreeable.'

Tom went over to him and explained the situation in English. The other man came and thanked me. He told me to sit down at my ease, look at the clock that was in front of me and not to move my head east or west, north or south. I did as requested.

He started drawing and scratching and then the door opened and a man came in. When he saw me with such a serious look on my face he saluted me. Who was it but Tadhg Ó Cíomháin from Cuas! He thought it strange that I didn't look at him and told me so too.

'In God's name, Tadhg,' I said, 'leave me alone for a while because I'm tied up.'

After a while the artist told me that he had completed the picture and I was free to look in any direction I liked and to talk.

The fee I got for having my picture drawn was just one pint. But, may God look down on us, whatever he did with my face – and I admit that it isn't too nice – the picture frightens me any time I look at it in Tom's bar. The worst part of all is the nose he gave me. It is the living image of the Scabby Rock.

23
CASTEL GANDOLFO

One of the most unusual things that happened here for a long time was the making of the film *Ryan's Daughter.* Most of it was made up on the Meelin, the hill above Graigue, and that is where all the action took place.

Before I went to America and for years afterwards there was nothing only heather and furze on the Meelin and when I came home I couldn't believe my eyes when I saw a village where there hadn't been a house or home before that. Kirrary was the name they gave it.

Although it was only a mock village it had everything that one might find in any village. It included a chapel but the Blessed Sacrament wasn't in it, I fear. Across the road from the chapel there was a real bar and if you went in, whether you had money or not, you were asked what sort of drink you wanted. There was also a police barracks and a lot of dwelling houses. To look at the place today you would swear that there was never a village there because no sooner had the filming finished than all the buildings were knocked to the ground.

Be that as it may *Ryan's Daughter* left a fortune of money in the area. Both young and old gained from it. The fellow who was cute put the money under a stone but the fellow who wasn't threw it to the wind, and there were many such people, unfortunately. I myself spent a month or so working there, if you could call it work. Everyone got three meals a day and that was the food that looked nice and tasted nice. On my first day at work there, before I had done a stroke, to my amazement I was handed four pounds, and the notes were so new that they rustled in my pocket. Unfortunately they weren't long in my pocket because what comes easily goes foolishly. It has always been the same with my money. It went with the wind as does the bark of a dog, with the result that I spent most of my life low in funds.

Ryan's Daughter helped greatly in putting this area on its feet but it wasn't the only thing that helped. All the people of this place have made millions out of visitors and students of Irish, and more luck to them. Looking around me I see wealth, I see riches, I see grand new houses and household appliances as fine as are to be found in the middle of Dublin. There are farm implements that the people of my age never even dreamt of. There is so much food and grub that people stuff themselves and I have always heard that it is a sin to eat too much. There are telephones in houses that didn't even have a tongs fifty years ago. People have cars instead of donkeys and there was a time when some of them didn't even have a donkey because they couldn't afford the tackling for him. There was no question of having a horse because it cost money to put one shoe on a horse, not to mind four, and many blacksmiths died without ever getting the money due to them because they were told after shoeing the horse, 'I'll pay you tomorrow,' but tomorrow never came.

Of course I am delighted to see this progress. In spite of all the wealth, though, I have a feeling that the people of today are not as happy or as kind-hearted as those who went before them and who never experienced anything but poverty. People are independent now and the neighbours don't help out as they used to. But thank God there are still fine people in the locality.

I saw nothing but poverty when growing up. Nevertheless I am not at all jealous of the young people today because I know that they too have their own problems. In a way I pity them. There is plenty of money in the pocket of every boy and girl going into a shop but they have more temptations to face up to than I and the likes of me had, and money more than anything else is the cause of those temptations. It brings nothing but trouble and strife.

Many kinds of people come to this locality, especially in the past few years, some of them through sheer love of the Irish language and others, I am afraid, who don't give a damn about it. From what I saw of them, and I have seen a lot, I believe that many of the students today know very little Irish. However I do not think we should blame them but rather the schools and colleges which they attend. Many of them come to me to improve their knowledge of the language and I do my best for them, but sometimes I cannot say for certain if they come for the sake of the language or for their own sake. The old saying tells us that the cat purrs only in its own interest. Be that as it may I have a welcome for all of them.

One day when I was in reasonably good health I was earthing potatoes back in Gearóid's Field. The sun was splitting the stones and I was pouring sweat because of the work. Then I saw this fellow clearing the stick that was across the gap. He had a white plastic bag in his hand.

'Good,' I said to myself, 'God's help is at hand. The plastic bag is a great sign. It won't be long before my thirst is quenched.'

I threw away the spade and sat down on the potato-bed. He sat down beside me. He took up the white bag. He put his hand down into it as far as his elbow. The first thing that came out was a biro and then a notebook! God forgive me, I said a prayer in my heart, and it was well for him that he didn't hear it, because if he had he would have taken to his heels and wouldn't dare look back.

He was a man who was trying to learn Irish and had got quite a lot of help from me prior to that. There are two kinds of people, some of them who are very thankful, and others who are not. It is not that I or people like me want any payment, but yet it is difficult to understand those who having got assistance show you only the back of their hand. With them it is a case of 'Goodbye!'

I am in great demand, especially in the summer, by friends who come to me year after year to learn Irish. They have been told that I am a great speaker of Irish, and really I have only a smattering compared to the old people. All the same, little and all as I have, I am glad to help anyone who I think is keen on learning it.

Not many visitors come to this locality in the winter. That means that I rarely have much company. Usually I get up very late. I spend most of the day sitting down thinking to myself. I have no interest in television except when a football or hurling match is being shown. When the night comes I might go to

Ballyferriter or again I might stay at home with my two sisters. Only for those same two I would be in a bad way and it is only right that I sing their praises because of their kindness, their good nature and above all their patience with me.

I have an old caravan just in front of the house. I call it Castel Gandolfo because I spend the summer living in it. When I sit down on a chair inside the door of that caravan my heart opens with joy because I see before me the nicest view in all the world. There I see the Big Raven Rock and the Raven's Mother, the Small Sound and Sybil Head. I see Clogher's White Strand below me, and if it were anywhere else in the world there wouldn't be room for all the people going down there. I look east to Coosnanay where there used to be twelve currachs in the days of the great fishermen and now there is only my own little one, the Star of the Sea, all on its own. I can see the Three Sisters, Smerwick Harbour, Mount Brandon and all the other places in this locality so dear to my heart.

Another thing I love to see is the gannet flying a hundred feet or more above the water. Then when he sees the fish underwater he dives straight down like a bullet out of a gun. I often watch the hawk too, perched still in the air with his two wings spread out. He sees the chicken or the frog down below him and he dives.

It has always been said that the three sharpest sights of all are the gannet's sight, the hawk's sight and Cully's sight. According to the story I heard Cully was a man who lived on the Western Island long ago. It was customary for the women of the Island at that time to go to Ballyferriter to buy provisions for the house. The men used to bring them to Dunquin in their currachs, put them ashore at Mor's Cliff and then go home. The women would walk up through Carhoo, down through the Gap of Graigue, and take the short cut through the top of the fields to Teeravane and from there to Ballyferriter.

When the men returned to the Island they went back to their work, but there was one man, Cully, and his job was to get a chair, take it outside the door of a certain house and sit on it. As soon as the women appeared at the top of the hill on their way home from the north, Cully would give a big loud shout:

'They're coming! They're at the Gap of Graigue, and my own wife has a bag on her back with a red twine around it.'

The men would then put the currachs on the water and go out again to Mor's Cliff for the women. It is said that that was the origin of the phrase 'Cully's sight'.

The view from Graigue hasn't changed since the day I was born but I have changed. True enough I have travelled quite a lot of the world and people were often jealous of me as they watched me going off, especially those who never went further east than the town of Dingle, but they don't really need to be jealous because they were a lot happier than I was. When they thought that I was in the prime of life and full of high spirits they were mistaken because I know all about myself and what I have gone through. Maybe if I too stayed at home I might be a lot better than I am, but there is no point in talking about that now. We must be satisfied.

I have my own faults. I have plenty of them, and being fond of the drink is the worst. In that way I am very like Matt Talbot, the poor workman from Dublin whose lodgings I visited long ago, and who lived a life of misery until he got the graces. Matt was found dead on the side of the street with chains around his body to torture himself. I have a picture of him and I pray regularly to him to put me on the right road just as God put Matt himself on the right road, so that the day will come when I can say that I ended up as he did and saved my soul.

I often lose heart, but bad and all as I am I have great trust in God because He is merciful and I know that he will show me mercy provided I ask him.

I have, and always had, great faith too in the Blessed Virgin because I believe that she brought the Saviour into the world and that so she is our mother. No wonder then that often during the day when I am on my own I say this prayer:

O Virgin Mary, O Mother Mary,
Set me on the right road.
Protect me on sea and land,
Protect me from the flagstones of hell.

May the angels be on guard above me,
God before me and God with me.

I trust in St Anthony above any other saint because ever since the day I found out that such a saint existed I never made a request to him that was not answered.

When I am bound for eternity, whenever that is, if I get the chance to speak I will say, 'O Virgin Mary, O Mother Mary, receive me.'

I am confident that she will.

LETTERS FROM THE GREAT BLASKET

EIBHLÍS NÍ SHÚILLEABHÁIN

This selection of *Letters from the Great Blasket,* for the most part written by Eibhlís Ní Shúilleabháin of the island to George Chambers in London, covers a period of over twenty years. Eibhlís married Seán Ó Criomhthain – a son of Tomás Ó Criomhthain, An tOileánach (The Islandman). On her marriage she lived in the same house as the Islandman and nursed him during the last years of his life which are described in the letters. Incidentally, the collection includes what must be an unique specimen of the Islandman's writing in English in the form of a letter expressing his goodwill towards Chambers.

Beginning in 1931 when the island was still a place where one might marry and raise a family (if only for certain exile in America) the letters end in 1951 with the author herself in exile on the mainland and 'the old folk of the island scattering to their graves'. By the time Eibhlís left the Blasket in July 1942 the island school had already closed and the three remaining pupils 'left to run wild with the rabbits'.

MÉINÍ
THE BLASKET NURSE

LESLIE MATSON

This is the life story of a remarkable woman, Méiní Dunlevy. Born in Massachusetts of Kerry parents, Méiní was reared in her grandparents' house in Dunquin. When she was nineteen she eloped with an island widower to the Great Blasket, where she worked as a nurse and midwife for thirty-six years. Returning widowed to Dunquin she died in 1967, aged 91.

Méiní's story, recorded by the author from her own accounts and those of her friends and relatives in Dunquin, is an evocation of a forceful, spicy personality and a compelling reconstruction of a way of life that has exercised an enduring fascination for readers. *Méiní, the Blasket Nurse* is a worthy successor to *An tOileánach* and *Twenty Years a-Growing*.

THE DAYS OF THE SERVANT BOY

LIAM O'DONNELL

'A day of great importance' – so Liam O'Donnell describes the time of the yearly hiring fair. A well-known feature of Irish farming life in his youth, it seems now a throwback to the distant past.

Though Liam O'Donnell's account of the days of the servant boy deals with the practice in County Cork the basic idea was the same throughout the country: the bonding of labouring men and women to farmers for a fixed term at a 'paltry' rate.

The author as a farmer's son was in an ideal position to describe the lives these hirelings had to lead with long hours, back-breaking work and often primitive living conditions.

His account is lively, often funny – for the story was not all gloom – and the reader is presented with an unforgettable picture of one of our Irish yesterdays, and left with the same great admiration that the author feels for the people he portrays so well.

BLESS 'EM ALL
THE LANES OF CORK

EIBHLÍS DE BARRA

'It has always been said that to qualify as a true Corkonian one must be able to boast of a least one city-born grandmother'. Eibhlís de Barra can justifiably lay claim to that distinction as both her grandmothers were natives of Cork. In 1939, shortly before the outbreak of war, her family moved into a house in Gunpowder Lane, paying rent of four shillings a week.

They quickly got to know everybody in Gunpowder Lane and became aware of the wonderful community spirit that existed amongst the families who lived there. The area all round them was a maze of lanes many of which have long since disappeared. In this nostalgic book Eibhlís de Barra clearly recalls Coburn's Lane, Fuller's Lane, Brandy Lane known today as St Finbar's Road and the many other lanes whose names never fail to awaken an intense feeling of nostalgia in the many fine people who spent their young days in them and grew up to live in better conditions.

In *Bless 'em All* the author describes the poverty, hunger and unemployment that dogged the people of working class Cork. The men and women in the lanes were prepared to turn their hand to anything to make a few shillings. In spite of sometimes overwhelming poverty parents made every effort to ensure that their children got the best food they could afford.

A fascinating and poignant story of life in Cork over sixty years ago.

LETTERS FROM IRISH COLLEGE

EDITED BY ROSE DOYLE

Do you remember being in Irish college in Spiddal, Ring, Muiríoch or Gortahork? Or your children leaving home alone for the first time and going west or south?

Irish college is a unique rite of passage for Irish adolescents. It is where they first experience homesickness, friendships they may keep for life, first love, the value of money and the great crack of céilís.

This collection, which spans the years 1936 to 1995, includes several letters from Ring in County Waterford written in Irish and English by former Taoiseach Garret FitzGerald, and dozens more from people, famous and not so famous, from all walks of Irish life.